סִייַעְתָּא לִגְמָרָא

AIDS TO
TALMUD
STUDY

by

Aryeh Carmell

Fourth Edition
newly revised and expanded

THE EAST END JEWISH SCHOLARSHIP CENTRE

FELDHEIM
Jerusalem / New York

Distributed by:

Feldheim Publishers Ltd
POB 6525
Jerusalem

Philipp Feldheim Inc.
96 East Broadway
New York, NY 10002

J. Lehmann
20 Cambridge Terrace
Gateshead, England

ISBN 0-87306-181-0

Published by
FELDHEIM PUBLISHERS
in conjunction with the
East End Jewish Scholarship Centre
London, England

Printed in Israel

C O N T E N T S

PREFACE TO THE FIRST EDITION

The first part of this booklet, "Gemara Key Words and Phrases", has already run through five editions in duplicated form and has provided very welcome assistance to beginners in the study of the Talmud. This is its first appearance in print. It has been extensively revised and the Aramaic and Hebrew appear for the first time with vowel points. The endeavour has been made to give a reasonably correct vocalisation of the Aramaic, but where the pronunciation current in the Yeshivos differs from this, the latter has often been indicated. The second part, "Commonly Used Abbreviations", has been revised, extended, vocalised and translated.

I would like to use this opportunity to express to my colleagues at the East End Jewish Scholarship Centre and Moreah Teachers' College, London, and particularly to my esteemed friend the Hon. Principal, Herman Zvi Sipper, Esq., my heartfelt appreciation of their outstanding educational work. Their greatest reward lies in the numbers of young people they have introduced to the study of Torah and Talmud and the practice of the laws and ideals which they teach; and who have then gone on to lead full and happy lives as committed, God-fearing Jews. May the Almighty continue to bless their efforts with success.

The world-wide re-awakening of interest in Judaism among our youth leads me to hope that more and more will join those who are already finding their way back to the Talmud — the unique source of both the intellectual alertness and the spiritual vigour of our people. And when they do, I venture to hope that this little book may serve to ease their onward path.

ARYEH CARMELL

Jerusalem, Kislev 5731

5

NOTE TO THE SECOND EDITION

The welcome given to this little work has been gratifying. This second edition has been carefully revised and extended, and includes two new features:

(1) A section on Talmudic Aramaic; this is a brief outline of Aramaic grammar with special reference to the colloquial forms found in the Babylonian Talmud.*

(2) An Appendix on the Tannaim and Amoraim, comprising historical charts displaying the main Tannaim and Amoraim and their inter-relationships, as well as an alphabetical index enabling the student to locate any name on the charts. A few notes on the correct vocalisation of Hebrew have also been appended.

My sincere thanks to all who have come forward with corrections and other suggestions for improvement; particularly to my son ר' יעקב מרדכי ישראל נ״י and my son-in-law ר' יעקב יהושע זאקס נ״י for their help; my son ר' אברהם חיים נ״י who suggested most of the new entries in the Key-word section; and my sons דוד יהודה נ״י and ר' יוסף אליהו נ״י for their helpful suggestions. Last by not least I thank my students at Yeshivat Dvar Yerushalayim (The Jerusalem Academy of Jewish Studies) whose enthusiasm provided the main stimulus for this new, expanded edition. Among these, special thanks are due to Mr. Shimon (Steve) Hurwitz, B.A., LL.B., for his help in preparing the charts of Tannaim and Amoraim.

A.C.

Jerusalem, Tevet 5734

---

* (A synopsis of Talmud Grammar may be found in Vol. VII of Blackman's Mishnayoth. This has been found useful and due acknowledgement is gladly made.)

NOTE TO THE FOURTH EDITION

The popularity of this little book is a sign of the times. We may be thankful that more and more people are indeed turning to the living sources of Torah, and finding their true selves in the process.

This edition, in addition to being carefully revised (and in this connection thanks are due to my youngest son אליעזר שלמה נ״י), also contains much new material: the first English translation of Rabbi Samuel Ha-Nagid's *Introduction to the Talmud,* which seems to have been written for a generation in some ways very similar to ours; and — in response to many requests — tables of Talmudic weights, measures, and monetary units, together with some indication of their purchasing power.

Good learning!

A.C.

Elul 5739

GEMARA KEY WORDS AND PHRASES

NOTE

This list is not a dictionary. It includes only those words and phrases which recur with considerable frequency in the Gemara, which are in fact the "operator words" of the Talmudic argument.

The order is strictly alphabetical, based on the phrase as a whole. Thus איהו comes after אי בעית אימא but before אי הכי. The entries inset in smaller type illustrate the use of the word or phrase forming the main entry.

The following abbreviations are used:

Ar. = Aramaic

abbr. = abbreviation

abbr. fr. = abbreviated from

contr. = contraction

cp. = compare

Heb. = Hebrew

lit. = literally

opp. = opposite

usu. pron. = usually pronounced

א

on; at; with reference to	־אַ
but	אֲבָל
on account of; subsidiary to; casually	אַגַּב
by the way	דֶּרֶךְ אַגַּב
acquisition (of chattels) as subsidiary (to land)	קִנְיָן אַגַּב
while; rather than	־אַדְּ
while he was going	אַדְּקָא אָזֵיל
rather than go in by that way, let him go in by the other	אַדְּעַיֵּיל בְּהָא לְעַיֵּיל בְּהָא
meanwhile	אַדְּהָכִי וְהָכִי
on the contrary	אַדְּרַבָּא
against one another	אֲהַדָּדֵי
on which?	אַהַיָּיא
set up; establish	אוֹקֵי, אוֹקִים
setting; particular application (determination of special circumstances or conditions under which statement in Mishna or Beraitha holds good)	אוּקִימְתָּא
you have established it	אוֹקִימְתָּא (אוֹקִימְתָּהּ)
to what (special case) have you applied (restricted) it?	בְּמַאי אוֹקִימְתָּהּ
they go according to their reason	אָזְדוּ לְטַעֲמַייהוּ
go	אָזֵיל
it is the same whether ... or ...	...אֶחָד... אֶחָד...
because of; on account of	אַטּוּ(1)
do you think?	אַטּוּ(2)
if	אִי (Ar.)
not	אִי (Heb.)

9

if it was said (at all), it was said like this	אִי אִיתְּמַר הָכִי אִיתְּמַר
it is all right if you say	אִי אָמְרַתְּ בִּשְׁלָמָא
impossible	אִי אֶפְשַׁר
they (the Bnei Yeshivah) asked	אִיבַּעְיָא לְהוּ
he should have; he asked	אִיבָּעֵי לֵיהּ
if you like I can say	אִי בָּעִית אֵימָא
both; in both cases	אִידֵי וְאִידֵי
the other (one) (usu. pron. אִידָךְ)	אִידַךְ
he; she	אִיהוּ, אִיהִי
if so	אִי הָכִי
since; because	אַיְידֵי דְ־
is concerned with	אַיְירֵי בְּ־
there is; there are (abbr. of אִית הָכָא	אִיכָּא
there is (this difference) between them	אִיכָּא בֵּינַיְיהוּ
some say	אִיכָּא דְאָמְרֵי
one can say	אִיכָּא לְמֵימַר
if; whereas	אִילוּ
if you were to say	אִילֵימָא
onwards, further	אֵילַךְ
say; I can say	אֵימָא
when; I should say; I could say	אֵימוּר
I admit that	אֵימוּר דְ־
if that were the only thing it would not be so difficult	אִי מִשּׁוּם הָא לָא אִירַיָא
when	אֵימַת
yes (usu. pronounced אִין (הֵן) אֵין to distinguish from 'not')	אֵין, אִין
quite so; yes; that is the case	אִין הָכִי נַמִי

10

does it not follow?	אֵינוֹ דִין
is it so? can it be?	אֵינִי
or, also; alternatively	אִי נַמִי (1)
even if	אִי נַמִי (2)
turn it round (change round the names)	אֵיפּוּךְ
shall I turn it round?	אֵיפּוּךְ אֲנָא
the opposite; the other way round	אִיפְּכָא
just the contrary appears to follow	אִיפְּכָא מִסְתַּבְרָא
it is necessary	אִיצְטְרִיךְ, אִיצְטְרִיכָא
there is; it is; it says	אִיתָא, אִית (יֵשׁ)
he holds	אִית לֵיה
he asked against him (from a Mishna or Beraitha, as follows)	אֵיתִיבֵיה
he is; it is; it applies	אִיתֵיה
if you want to say; some say	אִיתֵימָא (אִיתֵימָא .usu. pron)
it has been said (by an Amora)	אִיתַּמַר (אִיתְּמַר .usu. pron)
it was stated thereon	אִיתַּמַר עֲלָה
they are; there are	אִיתְנְהוּ
still; yet	אַכַּתֵּי
but	אֶלָּא
(following a refutation) But (we must adopt another ex- planation, viz.) Rabbi ... says	אֶלָּא אָמַר ר'
unless	אֶלָּא אִם כֵּן
but is it not ... ?	אֶלָּא לָאו
what then (is the interpretation)?	אֶלָּא מַאי
but according to that (it follows...)	אֶלָּא מֵעַתָּה

according to (lit., after the heart of...)	אַלִּיבָּא דְּ־
so we see	אַלְמָא
why	אַלָּמָה
if it were not	אִלְמָלֵא
if it were	אִלְמָלֵי
why? for what? on what?	אֲמַאי
if it be so	אִם אִיתָא
if Rav's Din is correct	אִם אִיתָא לְדְרַב
for that very reason	אַמְטוּ לְהָכִי
I should say; I could say; I can say; I said	אָמִינָא
(he) said	אֲמַר
said Abaye: (a new statement)	אָמַר אַבַּיֵי
Abaye said: (offering an alternative to the preceding statement)	אַבַּיֵי אָמַר
they (the B'nei Yeshiva) said; answered	אָמְרֵי
some say	אָמְרֵי לָהּ
he could answer you	אָמַר לָךְ
the Master said (referring back to previous quotation)	אֲמַר מַר
if you can say; if you accept that; granted that	אִם תִּמְצֵי לוֹמַר
I; we	אֲנָא, אֲנַן
also; even	אַף
we have also learnt this (in a Mishna)	אַף אֲנַן נַמִּי תְּנִינָא
although	אַף עַל גַּב
although	אַף עַל פִּי

nevertheless	אֲפִילוּ הָכִי
even if you say; you can even say	אֲפִילוּ תֵּימָא
possible	אֶפְשָׁר
to compare; equate	אַקּוּשֵׁי
we find	אַשְׁכְּחַן
it is found	אִשְׁתַּכַּח
he, it, came	אָתָא
came; he came; he has come	אָתָאִי
we came; we have come	אֲתָאן
you (pl.)	אַתּוּן
comes (m., f.)	אָתֵי, אָתְיָא
it comes (is derived) by a Kal Vachomer	אָתְיָא בְּקַל וָחוֹמֶר
it comes out all right	אָתֵי שַׁפִּיר

ב

on its own	בְּאַפֵּי נַפְשֵׁיהּ
their dispute is on this point	בְּהָא קָמִיפַּלְגֵי
(usu. pron. קָמִיפְּלְגֵי)	
while, together with	בַּהֲדֵי
together; equivalent(ly); among themselves	בַּהֲדֵי הֲדָדֵי
clearly, explicitly	בְּהֶדְיָא
whether . . . or . . .	בֵּין... בֵּין...
in between; the difference; in the meantime	בֵּינִי בֵּינִי
two people; a pair	בֵּי תְּרֵי
without cause; for nothing; incidentally	בִּכְדִי

13

without that	בְּלָאו הָכִי
in what (special case) have you established it?	בְּמַאי אוֹקִימְתָּא
ask; enquire; require; need; ought;	בָּעֵי
R. Zera asks	בָּעֵי ר׳ זֵירָא
he asked of him	בְּעָא מִינֵּיהּ
mere; merely; somewhere; anywhere; elsewhere; generally	בְּעַלְמָא
less than	בְּצִיר מ־
certain	בָּרִי
I am sure	בָּרִי לִי
Beraitha (mishnaic material not included in R. Yehuda Ha-Nassi's Mishna)	בָּרַיְיתָא
it is all right	בִּשְׁלָמָא
it is all right if you say	אִי אֲמַרְתְּ בִּשְׁלָמָא
(to be read) as a question	בִּתְמִיָּה
after	בָּתַר
the last	בַּתְרָא

ג

relating to; in connection with	גַּבֵּי
the thing itself; (introducing new passage of Gemara) (to treat of) the thing itself (=the matter just quoted)	גּוּפָא
surely this is self-contradictory?	הָא גּוּפָא קַשְׁיָא
learn	גָּמֵיר
a man should first accumulate knowledge and only then consider reasons	לִיגְמַר אִינַשׁ וַהֲדַר לִיסְבַּר
tradition; learning	גְּמָרָא

we learn	גַּמְרִינָן
drawing along; association	גְּרָרָא
brought in by association	אַגַּב גְּרָרָא נְסָבָה

ד

that (rel. pron.); of; because	דְּ־, דִּ־
this (f.)	דָּא
because	דְּהָא
place	דּוּכְתָּא
exact; exactly	דַּוְקָא
enough	דַּי
my; mine; me	דִּידִי
in my (his) opinion	לְדִידִי (לְדִידֵיהּ)
his	דִּידֵיהּ
this is his own opinion, that is his Teacher's	הָא דִּידֵיהּ הָא דְּרַבֵּיהּ
it is enough for him/it	דַּיּוֹ
(1) judge; (2) it is enough for them	דַּיָּן
derive; be exact	דַּיֵּיק
perhaps	דִּילְמָא, דִּלְמָא
law; judgement; a derivation (usually by Kal Vachomer)	דִּין
is it not a Kal Vachomer?	וְדִין הוּא
this (m)	דֵּין
that which he did; when it has already been done;	דִּיעֲבַד (דִּיעֶבַד)
you can also deduce it (from)	דַּיְקָא נַמִּי
take away	דַּל

of what; from what	דְּמַאי(1)
produce on which there is a doubt concerning separation of Maaser (tithe)	דְּמַאי (2)
resembles	דָּמֵי [דְּמִי .usu. pron]
it is as if it were burnt	כִּשְׂרוּף דָּמֵי
money	דָּמִי, דְּמֵי (דָּמִים, דָּמִין abr. of)
of the world; common, usual	דְּעָלְמָא
(to be) particular; exact	דָּק
he has not been precise	לָא דָק
he who compares it, how does he come to compare it?	דְּקָאָרֵי לָה מַאי קָאָרֵי לָה

ה

so; behold; surely	הָא (1)
did we not establish it?	הָא אוֹקִימְנָא
so, if it were not like this	הָא לָאו הָכִי
this (demons. pron.)	הָא(2)
one thing depends on the other	הָא בְּהָא תַּלְיָא
(גּוּפָא see under)	הָא גּוּפָא קַשְׁיָא
this (Din, saying) of R . . .	הָא דְּר׳...
both cases	הָא וְהָא
each case as applicable	הָא כִּדְאִיתָא וְהָא כִּדְאִיתָא
who is this? (which Tanna is the author of this?)	הָא מַנִּי
(התינח see under)	הָא תִּינַח
that (demonstr. pron.)	הַאי, הַהוּא
nowadays	הָאִידְנָא

16

how; that one, the other one	הָאֵיךְ
what is this? (somewhat disdainful rejection of foregoing)	הַאי מַאי
whosoever; a certain person; someone; anyone	הַאי מַאן
did he not say	הָאָמַר
afterwards; again	הָדַר
he retracted	הָדַר בֵּיהּ
that; a certain	הַהוּא
a certain man; that man (also used euphemistically of oneself)	הַהוּא גַבְרָא
since; because	הוֹאִיל וְ־
it was, he was; would be	הֲוָה
I would have said	הֲוָה אֲמִינָא
he should have	הֲוָה לֵיהּ לְ־
it was (f.); she was; would be	הֲוְיָא
we asked; we were	הֲוֵינַן
which?	הֵי
that one	הֵיאַךְ
that is (identical with)	הַיְינוּ
this is the same thing	הַיְינוּ הַךְ
Rabbi Y's (statement) seems to be identical with (that of) the first Tanna	ר׳ יוֹסֵי הַיְינוּ תַּנָּא קַמָּא
where	הֵיכָא, הֵיכָן
how?	הֵיכִי
how is that to be understood; in what case? what is a practical illustration of . . . ?	הֵיכִי דָמֵי
in what case can this be found?	הֵיכִי מִשְׁכַּחַת לָהּ
the halacha; the final decision	הִילְכְתָא

that (demonstr. pron.)	הַךְ
comparison; equation	הֶיקֵשׁ
here	הָכָא
what are we dealing with here?	הָכָא בְּמַאי עַסְקִינָן
thus; so	הָכִי
that is so	הָכִי נַמִי
so it also follows by reasoning; so it appears reasonable	הָכִי נַמִי מִסְתַּבְּרָא
therefore	הִלְכָךְ
these	הַנֵּי
these words (apply)	הַנֵּי מִילֵי
those	הַנָךְ
now	הַשְׁתָּא
that is all right	הַתִּינַח (הָא תִּינַח)
there; elsewhere	הָתָם

ו

and the other? (what does he say about the argument?)	וְאִידַךְ (וְאִידָךְ) (usu. pron.
whereas	וְאִילוּ
that which you found difficult	וּדְקַקְשְׁיָא לָךְ
but surely	וְהָא
did you not say?	וְהָאֲמַרְתְּ
provided that	וְהוּא
and we asked on it	וְהָוֵינָן בָּהּ
but surely we have learnt in a Beraitha ... ?; (more rarely) and so we have learnt in a Beraitha	וְהָתַנְיָא

18

can it really be (that)	וְכִי
nothing	וְלֹא כְלוּם
he has done nothing at all	לֹא עָשָׂה וְלֹא כְלוּם
and according to your reason (opinion) (is it any better)?	וּלְטַעְמֵךְ
if even (introductory clause of Kal Vachomer)	וּמַה
what then is to be learnt here (that could give occasion to the verse) to say . . .	וּמַה תַּלְמוּד לוֹמַר
some bring it in the name of R . . .	וּמָטוּ בָּה מִשּׁוּם דר'
and I will suggest an apparent contradiction	וּרְמִינְהִי (וְרָמֵי אֲנָא אַהֲאי)
and further; and again	וְתוּ
and nothing more; (= this is the end of the argument)	וְתוּ לָא מִידֵי
does this really follow?	וְתִיסְבְּרָא
why not derive it from . . . ?	וְתֵיפּוּק לֵיהּ

ז

this means; this implies	זֹאת אוֹמֶרֶת
sell (3rd. pers. sing. past)	זַבִּין
buy (3rd. pers. sing. past)	זְבַן
this, and needless to say, that (=the cases are in ascending order of demonstrability)	זוֹ, וְאֵין צָרִיךְ לוֹמַר זוֹ
go!	זִיל

19

ח

"firstly and furthermore" (one out of several cases, reasons, etc.)	חֲדָא וְעוֹד
we see	חֲזֵינַן
obliged; liable	חַיָּיב
the Mishna is deficient, and should be read as follows	חַסּוֹרֵי מֵיחַסְּרָא וְהָכִי קָתָנֵי

ט

many; plenty; well	טוּבָא
the reason	טַעֲמָא
the reason is because	טַעֲמָא דְּ־
more	טְפֵי
more than	טְפֵי מִ־

י

gives	יָהֵיב
it is possible; I might think	יָכוֹל
learn; derive (it)	יַלֵּיף (לָהּ)
derivation	יַלְפּוּתָא

כ

as if it were possible	כִּבְיָכוֹל
(1) when; as (Ar.); (2) jar (Heb.)	כַּד
as	כְּד־
as you said	כִּדְקָאָמַרְתְּ
like the statement of Rava	כִּדְרָבָא
so that	כְּדֵי

by the way; without special reason; anonymously	כְּדִי
it disappears without any formality	פָּקְעָה בִּכְדִי
he refers to it just by the way; without specific reason	כְּדִי נִסְבָה
as we answered	כִּדְשַׁנִּינָן
all	כּוֹלָא, כּוּלֵי
the whole world; everybody	כּוּלֵי עָלְמָא
all that much; so much	כּוּלֵי הַאי
like; as; when; if	כִּי
like that	כִּי הַאי
in that way; in that manner	כִּי הַאי גַוְונָא
if you say	כִּי תֵּימָא
just as; so that; in order that	כִּי הֵיכִי (דְ־)
since, because	כֵּיוָן (כֵּינָן .usu. pron)
when (=in which case) do they dispute	כִּי פְּלִיגֵי
so	כָּךְ
as long as; whenever	כָּל אֵימַת
is it within his powers?	כָּל כְּמִינֵיה
(1) nothing; (2) introducing a question	כְּלוּם
(1) he has done nothing	לֹא עָשָׂה כְּלוּם
(2) have you any pleasure?	כְּלוּם יֵשׁ לְךָ הֲנָאָה
as if to say; that is to say	כְּלוֹמַר
towards	כְּלַפֵּי
in which direction is this tending? (=is not your reasoning at fault?)	כְּלַפֵּי לַיָּיא
whatever the amount	כָּל שֶׁהוּא
all the more (so)	כָּל שֶׁכֵּן
as if; like the one; like whom?	כְּמַאן
	כְּמִינֵיה עי׳ כָּל כְּמִינֵיה

similar to	כְּעֵין
in the same way as . . .	כְּשֵׁם
(this is) similar to the (following) dispute of Tannaim	כְּתַנָּאֵי

ל

no; not; is it not? (usu. pron. as Hebrew: לֹא)	לָא
only	לֹא . . . אֶלָּא
it is only necessary	לֹא נִצְרְכָא אֶלָּא
is it not enough for them?	לֹא דַיָּין
is it not obvious?	לֹא כָּל שֶׁכֵּן
don't they dispute?	וְלָא פְּלִיגֵי
"not only this, even that" (= the cases in the Mishna are in descending order of demonstrability)	לֹא זוֹ אַף זוֹ
not so	לֹא כִי
nothing	לֹא כְּלוּם
not only; needless to say	לָא מִיבַּעְיָא
does the Master not hold . . . ?	לָא סָבַר מַר
you cannot think so	לָא סַלְקָא דַעְתָּךְ
no, it is necessary in the following case	לָא צְרִיכָא דְּ־
it is necessary (or applicable) only . . .	לָא צְרִיכָא אֶלָּא דְּ־
(there is) no difference	לָא שְׁנָא
this Mishna as learnt only . . . ; this Din applies only . . .	לֹא שָׁנוּ אֶלָּא
no; not; is it not?	לַאו
did we not learn thereon	לַאו אִיתְּמַר עֲלָהּ
very well; all's well	לְאַיֵּי
to include	לְאַתּוּיֵי

concerning; in connection with	לְגַבֵּי
further on; later; elsewhere	לְהַלָּן
let it be	לֶיהֱוֵי
let him fear	לֵיחוּשׁ
there is not; it is not; it is impossible	לֵיכָּא (לֵית הָכָא)
it is impossible to say so	לֵיכָּא לְמֵימַר הָכִי
let him say; let it (the verse) say; shall we say	לֵימָא
shall we say (that the foregoing is) like (the following dispute of) Tannaim	לֵימָא כְּתַנָּאֵי
let him distinguish; let him dispute	לִיפְלוֹג
why not incorporate the distinction in that very case	לִיפְלוֹג וְלֵיתְנֵי בְּדִידַהּ
expression; language; version	לִישָׁנָא
there is not; it is not (abbr.	לֵיתָא (לָא אִיתָא) לֵית
he does not hold (the opinion); he has not got	לֵית לֵיהּ
there is nothing in it for us; it does not matter	לֵית לָן בַּהּ
let the Mishna say	לִיתְנֵי
according to everybody	לְכוּלֵּי עָלְמָא
to begin with; the recommended course of action (opp. דִּיעֲבַד)	לְכַתְּחִלָּה
why do I need?	לָמָה לִי
to say; do you mean to say?	לְמֵימְרָא
to exclude (Ar.) לְמֵעוּטֵי (Heb.) לְמַעֵט	
after all; for ever	לְעוֹלָם
regarding	לְעִנְיַן
to include (Heb.) לְרַבּוֹת (Ar.) לְרִיבּוּיֵי	

23

מ

what	מַאי
what is the relevance of? why just . . . ?	מַאי אִירְיָא
what is there to say? what can you answer?	מַאי אִיכָּא לְמֵימַר
so what?	מַאי הֲוָה
what about it? what is the conclusion?	מַאי הֲוֵי עֲלָה
is it not the case? (what is the position? is it not . . . ?)	מַאי לָאו
what need is there to say (it)?	מַאי לְמֵימְרָא
how does it imply?	מַאי מַשְׁמַע
what difference does it make to him (us)?	מַאי נָפְקָא לֵיה (לָן) מִינַּהּ
what is he doing? what business has this here?	מַאי עֲבִדְתֵּיה
what is the difference?	מַאי שְׁנָא
what is the inference?	מַאי תַּלְמוּדָא
who; who is	מַאן
the one who says	מַאן דְּאָמַר
of whom have you heard?	מַאן שְׁמַעַתְּ לֵיה
who is the Tanna	מַאן תַּנָּא
needed	מִבָּעְיָא, מִיבָּעְיָא
(1) he should have (2) it should have said (in the verse) (3) it is needed	מִיבָּעְיָא לֵיה
"A"? it should have said "B"!	"א"? "ב" מִיבָּעְיָא לֵיה
since; because; out of;	מִגּוֹ, מִיגּוֹ(1)
one out of two	חֲדָא מִיגּוֹ תַּרְתֵּי
"because" (abbr. for a deductive principle)	מִגּוֹ, מִיגּוֹ(2)

we say "because" (= use this deductive principle)	אַמְרִינָן מִיגוֹ
since; following from the fact that . . .	מִדְּ־
what; what is; (introducing a clause of comparison) just as	מַה

just as his seed is alive so is he alive (lit. what is his seed? — Alive! So is he alive)	מַה זַרְעוֹ בַּחַיִּים אַף הוּא בַּחַיִּים
what about — . . . ? (introducing a refutation of a Kal Vachomer)	מַה לְ־

what difference is it to me?	מַה לִּי
where do you get it from? why should you assume?	מֵהֵיכָא תֵּיתֵי
what do we find? just as we find (first clause of a comparison)	מַה מָּצִינוּ
whatever you want; whichever way you turn	מָה נַפְשָׁךְ, מִמָּה נַפְשָׁךְ
what is it? what is the "din"?	מַהוּ (־מַה הוּא)
you might think; you might have thought	מַהוּ דְּתֵימָא
agrees, agree	מוֹדָה, מוֹדִים
it is clear; clearer; better	מֵחַוַּרְתָּא
(particle introducing a question)	מִי

are they alike? does this resemble the foregoing?	מִי דָמֵי
do we fear?	מִי חַיישִׁינָן
did he not say?	מִי לָא אָמַר
	מִיבַּעְיָא (ע׳ מִבַּעְיָא)

at once	מִיַּד
something; anything; at all; (introducing a rhetorical question) is it? do we?	מִידִי (־מִידַּעַם)

are they at all alike?	מִידִי אִירַיָא
does it then say "A" in the Mishna?	מִידִי "א" תְּנַן

something else	מִידִי אַחֲרִינָא
something like; this resembles . . .	מִידִי דְּהַוָּא אֵ׳
something	מִידַּעַם
however; at least	מִיהָא
but; however	מִיהוּ
at least; at any rate	מִיהַת
who says?	מִי יֵימַר
brings it; derives it	מַיְיתֵי לַהּ
thing	מִילְתָא
statement	מֵימְרָא
from him, from it	מִינֵיהּ
it follows; it appears to be reasonable (that)... מִיסְתַּבְּרָא	
exclusion	מִיעוּט
they dispute (usu. pron. מִיפַּלְגֵי) מִיפְלְגֵי	
they (the Bnei Yeshivah) asked; objected (from a Mishna or Beraitha)	מֵיתִיבֵי
since; because (usu. pron. מְכְדִי) מִכְּדִי	
anyway	מִכָּל מָקוֹם
it follows	מִכְּלַל
how do we know? from what?	מִמַּאי
of itself; by itself; automatically	מִמֵּילָא
from where	מְנָא
from where can I prove it?	מְנָא אַמִּינָא לַהּ
from where does he derive it?	מְנָא לֵיהּ
Whence can you derive it?	מְנָא תֵּימְרָא
who is he? (מַאן הוּא) מַנּוּ	
who is it? (מַאן הִיא) מַנִּי	
which Tanna is (the author of) our Mishna?	מַנִּי מַתְנִיתִין

26

from where?	מְנַיִן
it supports him	מְסַיֵּיע לֵיה
it follows; it appears to be reasonable (that) . . .	מִסְתַּבְּרָא
originally; from before; at 'first; from the origin	מֵעִיקָרָא
act; story; event; case	מַעֲשֶׂה
answer; solve difficulty (lit. take to pieces)	מְפָרֵק
to be able	מָצֵי
compares	מַקִּישׁ
to compare	אַקּוּשֵׁי
ask a question; raise a difficulty or objection	מַקְשֶׁה
the Master; the Rabbi; you (in polite speech)	מַר
one holds	מַר סָבַר
whatever it is; the smallest amount	מַשֶּׁהוּ (~מַה שֶׁהוּא)
makes; makes equivalent (see שׁוי)	מְשַׁוֵּי
because of	מִשּׁוּם(1)
in the name of	מִשּׁוּם(2)
in the name of	מִשְׁמֵיה דְּ~
it can be found; a case can be found	מִשְׁכַּחַת לָה
it means; it implies	מַשְׁמַע
it means this to him; it has this significance to him	מַשְׁמַע לֵיה
answer; reply to an objection	מְשַׁנֵּי
it (he) talks, speaks	מִשְׁתָּעֵי
carry on a court case with	מִשְׁתָּעֵי דִּינָא בַּהֲדֵי

27

the verse speaks of	בְּ... מִשְׁתָּעֵי קְרָא
from out of; from amongst	מִתּוֹךְ
(he) raised an objection from a Mishna or Beraitha	מָתֵיב
he asks it and he answers it	הוּא מָתֵיב לָהּ וְהוּא מְפָרֵק לָהּ
raise an objection (by counter-argument)	מַתְקֵיף

נ

let it be; assuming that	נְהִי
it is; he is	נִיהוּ
to him; to it	נִיהֲלֵיהּ
(it is) satisfactory	נִיחָא
let us fear	נֵיחוּשׁ
let us see	נֵיחֲזֵי אֲנַן
let us say	נֵימָא
they	נִינְהוּ
let it write	נִכְתּוֹב
also	נַמִי
he derives it (lit.: it comes out for him)	נַפְקָא לֵיהּ
the practical difference (lit. what comes out of it)	נַפְקָא מִינָהּ
take; adopt; use (a phrase etc.)	נָקַט, נָקֵיט

ס

exercise reasoning faculty (see נמיר)	סָבֵיר
he holds	סְבִירָא לֵיהּ

reason; reasoning; something arrived at by reasoning	סְבָרָא
he holds it; he holds in that connection	סְבַר לָהּ (סָבַר לָהּ .usu. pron)
he goes, it goes	סָגֵי
enough	סַגֵּי
connected passage of Gemara	סוּגְיָא
after all, ultimately	סוֹף סוֹף
argument in support; aid	סִיַּיעְתָּא
the last part	סֵיפָא
you might think; do you think? do you mean?	סַלְקָא דַעְתָּךְ
can you possibly mean...?	?סַלְקָא דַעְתָּךְ ...
you might think I should say	סַלְקָא דַעְתָּךְ אַמִינָא

ע

its business; its concern	עֲבִידְתָּהּ
what has it to do (here) what's its business?	מַאי עֲבִידְתָּהּ
case	עוּבְדָא
how much more so	עַל אַחַת כַּמָּה וְכַמָּה
through, by means of; on behalf of;	עַל יְדֵי
against your will; perforce (H.) עַל כָּרְחַךְ (.Ar)	עַל כָּרְחַיךְ
world	עָלְמָא
this world	הַאי עָלְמָא
that world (the world to come)	הַהוּא עָלְמָא
matter; connection	עִנְיָן
if it has no connection with ...	אם אֵינוֹ עִנְיָן לְ-
we are dealing (with)	עַסְקִינַן

29

פ

go out	פּוּק
go out and teach it outside (in public) or: go, expunge it	פּוּק תְּנִי לְבָרָא
a little	פּוּרְתָּא
disproof; refutation	פִּירְכָא
dispute	פְּלוּגְתָּא
disputes; divides (usu. pron. פָּלֵיג)	פָּלֵיג
a detail	פְּרַט
excluding . . .	פְּרַט לְ־
he asks; raises an objection (usu. pron. פְּרִיךְ)	פָּרֵיךְ
solve, answer (imperative)	פְּשׁוֹט
solve at least one (of the problems)	פְּשׁוֹט מֵיהָא חֲדָא
he answers; solves (usu. pron. פְּשִׁיט)	פָּשֵׁיט
surely it is obvious? (sometimes:) it is obvious that	פְּשִׁיטָא

צ

it is necessary	צְרִיכָא

ק

(a particle preceding or prefixed to a verb, denoting emphasis)	קָא, קָ־
it stands; it refers	קָאֵי (קָאֵים)
refers to	קָאֵי אַ־
it stands as it was	כִּדְקָאֵי קָאֵי
he/it lets us hear; tells us (this new point)	קָא מַשְׁמַע לָן
he said	קָאֲמַר (קָא אֲמַר)

30

you (we) might think at the moment; it might occur to you	קָא סַלְקָא דַעְתָּךְ (דַעְתִּין)
we hold	קַיְימָא לָן
they hold; they have established	קִים לְהוּ
inference from the weaker to the stronger (a minori)	קַל וָחוֹמֶר
first	קַמָּא
before him	קַמֵּיהּ
they dispute (usu. pron. קָמִיפְלְגִי) (־קָא מִיפַּלְגִי) קָמִיפַּלְגִי
	קָמַשְׁמַע לָן עי׳ קָא מַשְׁמַע לָן
Scripture	קְרָא
difficulty; objection; it is difficult	קַשְׁיָא
he learns	קָתָנֵי (קָא תָּנֵי)

ר

inclusion; an expression which includes more (in the Din)	רִבּוּי, רִיבּוּי
the All-merciful One; (the Author of) the Torah	רַחְמָנָא
the first part; beginning; head	רֵישָׁא
(he) raised an objection from a verse of Scripture; propounded an (apparent) contradiction between two verses or quotations	רָמֵי

ש

| for there is no inference to say ... (there is apparently nothing new to be learnt here, to warrant the verse saying) | שֶׁאֵין תַּלְמוּד לוֹמַר |

it is different	שָׁאנֵי
leave(s)	שָׁבֵיק
again	שׁוּב
equal; worth	שָׁוֵי
(he) made; made equivalent	שַׁוִּי
leave over; leave out	שַׁיֵּיר
what (else) has he left out that he should have left this out?	מַאי שַׁיֵּיר דְּהַאי שַׁיֵּיר
we hear; we understand	שַׁמְעִינָן
you can derive (it); infer it	שְׁמַע מִינָהּ
May we infer that the Halachah is like R....? We may	שְׁמַע מִינָהּ הִילְכְתָא כְּר'...? שְׁמַע מִינָהּ
something learnt; a piece of Gemara	שְׁמַעְתְּתָא
he answers it	שָׁנֵי לָהּ
well; it is good	שַׁפִּיר
it is all right	שַׁפִּיר דָּמֵי
takes	שָׁקֵיל

ת

come (and) hear (introducing an attempted proof)	תָּא שְׁמַע
(he) wondered at it	תָּהֵי בֵּיהּ
further; moreover	תּוּ (abbr. of תּוּב, Heb. שׁוּב)
it can (could) (should) be asked by you	תִּיבָּעֵי לָךְ
a refutation	תִּיוּבְתָּא
is this a refutation of Rava?	תִּיוּבְתָּא דְּרָבָא?
It is.	תִּיוּבְתָּא
you will say	תֵּימָא

surprising (introducing a question in Tosaphot) — תֵּימָה

all very well — תִּינַח

"A" is all very well, but what can one say about "B"? — תִּינַח "א", "ב" מַאי אִיכָּא לְמֵימַר

derive it — תֵּיפוֹק לֵיהּ

let it stand; the question must remain unanswered — תֵּיקוּ (תֵּיקוּם)

depends — תַּלְיָא

the thing depends on... — בְּ...תַּלְיָא מִילְתָא

an inference to say (= there is an inference to be drawn here, leading the verse to say) — תַּלְמוּד לוֹמַר

three; three things — תְּלַת

it was learnt; he learnt — תְּנָא

Tanna, Rabbi of Mishna times — תַּנָּא(1)

person who had memorised much Mishnaic material (in Gemara times) — תַּנָּא (2)

our Tanna (the Tanna of the Mishna) also learns like that — תַּנָּא תּוּנָא

condition — תְּנַאי

it is a dispute of Tannaim — תַּנָּאֵי הִיא

the Rabbis have learnt (in a Beraitha) — תָּנוּ רַבָּנָן (usu. pron. תְּנוּ רַבָּנָן)

he (the Tanna) learns (in a Mishna or Beraitha) — תָּנֵי(1)

he (i.e. an early Amora) learns (in his personal Mishna or Beraitha collection) — תָּנֵי(2)

Bar Kappara learnt a Baraitha (as follows) — תָּנֵי בַּר קַפָּרָא

33

Rav taught (the Mishna) to his son (in the following version)	תְּנֵי רַב לִבְרֵיהּ
it has been learnt (in a Beraitha)	תַּנְיָא
we have already learnt this in a Mishna	תְּנִינָא
we have learnt a Mishna in the same sense as the Beraitha	תְּנִינָא לְהָא דְתְנוּ רַבָּנָן
you have learnt it in the Mishna	תְּנִיתוּהָ
we have learnt (in a Mishna)	תְּנַן
we have learnt a Mishna elsewhere	תְּנַן הָתָם
he interpreted it	תִּרְגְּמָהּ
both of them	תַּרְוַויְיהוּ
two	תְּרֵי, תַּרְתֵּי
two (contradictory statements)?	תַּרְתֵּי

34

COMMONLY USED ABBREVIATIONS

רָאשֵׁי תֵּיבוֹת

א

impossible	אִי אֶפְשָׁר	א"א
it is all right if you say	אִי אֲמַרְתְּ בִּשְׁלָמָא	אא"ב
unless	אֶלָּא אִם כֵּן	אא"כ
if you like I can say	אִי בָּעֵית אֵימָא	אב"א
some say	אִיכָּא דְּאָמְרֵי	א"ד
or perhaps	אוֹ דִּילְמָא	
if so	אִי הָכִי	א"ה
quite so	אֵין הָכִי נַמִי	אה"נ
but certainly	אֶלָּא וַדַּאי	א"ו
the nations of the world	אוּמּוֹת הָעוֹלָם	אוה"ע
after this	אַחַר זֶה	אח"ז
afterwards	אַחַר כָּךְ	אח"כ
he said to him	אָמַר לוֹ, אֲמַר לֵיהּ	א"ל
or also	אִי נַמִי	א"נ
himself	אֶת עַצְמוֹ	א"ע
although	אַף עַל גַּב	אע"ג
but perforce	אֶלָּא עַל כָּרְחָךְ	אע"כ
although	אַף עַל פִּי	אע"פ
even so	אֲפִילוּ הָכִי	אפ"ה
even	אֲפִילוּ	אפי'
it is unnecessary	אֵינוֹ צָרִיךְ	א"צ
it is unnecessary to say	אֵינוֹ צָרִיךְ לוֹמַר	אצ"ל
the verse says	אָמַר קְרָא	א"ק
Rabbi . . . said	אָמַר רַבִּי...	א"ר

35

it comes out all right	אָתֵי שַׁפִּיר	א״ש
if you will say	אִם תֹּאמַר	א״ת
if you can assume	אִם תִּמְצֵי לוֹמַר	את״ל

ב

Bava Bathra	בָּבָא בַתְרָא	ב״ב
court	בֵּית דִּין	ב״ד
when is this said	בַּמֶּה דְבָרִים אֲמוּרִים	בד״א
the school of Hillel	בֵּית הִלֵּל	ב״ה
thank G-d	בָּרוּךְ הַשֵּׁם	
toilet	בֵּית הַכִּסֵּא	בה״כ
synagogue	בֵּית הַכְּנֶסֶת	בהכ״נ
grace after meals	בִּרְכַּת הַמָּזוֹן	בהמ״ז
Temple	בֵּית הַמִּקְדָּשׁ	בהמ״ק
twilight	בֵּין הַשְׁמָשׁוֹת	בה״ש
flesh and blood; mortal man	בָּשָׂר וָדָם	ב״ו
	בָּשָׂר וָדָם	בו״ד
at the present time	בַּזְּמַן הַזֶּה	בזה״ז
the synagogue	בֵּית הַכְּנֶסֶת	ביהכ״נ
in any place	בְּכָל מָקוֹם	בכ״מ
in several places	בְּכַמָּה מְקוֹמוֹת	
without that	בְּלָאו הָכִי	בלא״ה
without a vow	בְּלִי נֶדֶר	בל״נ
without a doubt	בְּלִי סָפֵק	בל״ס
Bava Metzia	בָּבָא מְצִיעָא	ב״מ
Noachide, non-Jew	בֶּן נֹחַ	ב״נ
people	בְּנֵי אָדָם	בנ״א
people of Israel	בְּנֵי יִשְׂרָאֵל	בנ״י

with the help of Heaven	בְּסִיַעְתָּא דִשְׁמַיָא	בס״ד
twice	ב׳ פְּעָמִים	ב״פ
house-owner	בַּעַל הַבַּיִת	בעה״ב
living things	בַּעֲלֵי חַיִּים	בע״ח
with G-d's help	בְּעֶזְרַת הַשֵׁם	בעז״ה
against his will	בְּעַל־כָּרְחוֹ	בע״כ
Bava Kamma	בָּבָא קַמָּא	ב״ק
Bereshit Rabba	בְּרֵאשִׁית רַבָּה	ב״ר
the school of Shammai	בֵּית שַׁמַּאי	ב״ש

ג

also	גַם כֵּן	ג״כ
the garden of Eden; Paradise	גַן עֵדֶן	ג״ע
forbidden marriages	גִּלוּי עֲרָיוֹת	
three times	ג׳ פְּעָמִים	ג״פ
similar expression	גְּזֵרָה שָׁוָה	ג״ש

ד

another explanation; another thing	דָּבָר אַחֵר	ד״א
all agree	דִּבְרֵי הַכֹּל	ד״ה
the passage commencing	דִּבּוּר הַמַּתְחִיל	
that he should have	דְּהֲוֵי לֵיה	דהו״ל

ה

I would have said	הֲוָה אַמִּינָא	ה״א
what are we dealing with here	הָכָא בְּמַאי עָסְקִינָן	הב״ע
this is how we read	הָכִי גַרְסִינָן	ה״ג

37

in what case?	הֵיכִי דָמֵי	ה״ד
that which you say	הָדָא דְּאַתְּ אֲמַר	הד״א
that is the same	הוּא הָדֵין	ה״ה
it is	הֲרֵי הוּא	
I would have thought	הֲוָה אֲמִינָא	הו״א
he should have; it would be	הֲוָה לֵיהּ	הו״ל
this is	הֲרֵי זֶה	ה״ז
that is the reason	הַיְינוּ טַעֲמָא	ה״ט
these words (apply)	הַנֵּי מִילֵי	ה״מ
the onus of proof is upon the claimant	הַמּוֹצִיא מֵחֲבֵרוֹ עָלָיו הָרְאָיָה	המע״ה
so also	הָכִי נַמִי	ה״נ
these words (apply)	הַנֵּי מִילֵי	הנ״מ
this is what he said	הָכִי קָאֲמַר	ה״ק
he asked	הִקְשָׁה	הק׳
the holy one	הַקָּדוֹשׁ	
G-d	הַקָּדוֹשׁ בָּרוּךְ הוּא	הקב״ה
G-d	הַשֵּׁם יִתְבָּרַךְ	הש״י

ו

etcetera	וְגוֹמֵר	וגו׳
and so on	וְכוּלֵי	וכו׳
furthermore one can say	וְעוֹד יֵשׁ לוֹמַר	ועוי״ל

ז

this means	זֹאת אוֹמֶרֶת	ז״א
this is not right	זֶה אֵינוֹ	
these are his words	זֶה לְשׁוֹנוֹ	ז״ל

38

his memory for a blessing	זִכְרוֹנוֹ לִבְרָכָה	ז״ל
the memory of the righteous is for a blessing	זֵכֶר צַדִּיק לִבְרָכָה	זצ״ל
that which the verse says	זֶה שֶׁאָמַר הַכָּתוּב	זש״ה

ח

G-d forbid	חַס וְחָלִילָה	ח״ו
the Sages say	חֲכָמִים אוֹמְרִים	חכ״א
deaf-mute, lunatic and minor	חֵרֵשׁ שׁוֹטֶה וְקָטָן	חש״ו

י

some say	יֵשׁ אוֹמְרִים	י״א
some read	יֵשׁ גּוֹרְסִין	י״ג
evil inclination	יֵצֶר הָרָע	יצה״ר
may He be blessed	יִתְבָּרַךְ	ית׳
may His name be blessed	יִתְבָּרַךְ שְׁמוֹ	ית״ש
one can say	יֵשׁ לוֹמַר	י״ל

כ

(he) wrote	כָּתַב	כ׳
each one	כָּל אֶחָד וְאֶחָד	כאו״א
high priest	כֹּהֵן גָּדוֹל	כה״ג
in that manner	כִּי הַאי גַּוְנָא	
all this	כָּל זֶה	כ״ז
all the time	כָּל זְמָן	
so much	כָּל כָּךְ	כ״כ
likewise	כְּמוֹ כֵן	
every place; anywhere	כָּל מָקוֹם	כ״מ

39

as it is written	כְּמוֹ שֶׁכָּתוּב	כמ״ש
as we have written	כְּמוֹ שֶׁכָּתַבְנוּ	
as mentioned above	כַּנִּזְכָּר לְעֵיל	כנ״ל
so it appears to me	כֵּן נִרְאֶה לִי	
everyone	כּוּלֵי עָלְמָא	כ״ע
so it should read	כֵּן צָרִיךְ לוֹמַר	כצ״ל
whatever the amount	כָּל שֶׁהוּא	
all the more	כָּל שֶׁכֵּן	כ״ש
all the more	כָּל שֶׁכֵּן	כש״כ

ל

language; expression	לָשׁוֹן	ל׳
another version	לִישְׁנָא אַחֲרִינָא	ל״א
from Creation: Anno Mundi	לִבְרִיאַת הָעוֹלָם	לבה״ע
we do not read	לָא גַּרְסִינָן	ל״ג
it does not resemble	לָא דָמֵי	ל״ד
it is not exact	לָאו דַּוְקָא	
complete denial	לֹא הָיוּ דְבָרִים מֵעוֹלָם	להד״ם
holy language	לְשׁוֹן הַקֹּדֶשׁ	לה״ק
slander	לְשׁוֹן הָרָע	לה״ר
according to everyone	לְכוּלֵי עָלְמָא	לכו״ע
he does not hold	לֵית לֵיהּ	ל״ל
why should I; why do I need	לָמָה לִי	
according to the one who says	לְמַאן דְּאָמַר	למ״ד
according to this	לְפִי זֶה	לפ״ז
according to what	לְפִי מַה	לפ״מ
Common Era	לִסְפִירַת הַנּוֹצְרִים	לסה״נ

40

it is not difficult	לָא קַשְׁיָא	ל״ק
the first version	לִישְׁנָא קַמָּא	ל״ק
it is not difficult at all	לָא קָשֶׁה מִידֵי	לק״מ
no difference	לֹא שְׁנָא	ל״ש
does not apply	לֹא שַׁיָּיךְ	
negative command	לֹא תַעֲשֶׂה	ל״ת

מ

the one who says	מַאן דְּאָמַר	מ״ד
you might have thought	מַהוּ דְּתֵימָא	
from the Torah	מִדְּאוֹרַיְיתָא	מדאו׳
from the Torah	מִן הַתּוֹרָה	מה״ת
what is the reason	מַאי טַעֲמָא	מ״ט
A parable. What does this resemble?	מָשָׁל לְמָה הַדָּבָר דּוֹמֶה	מלה״ד
negative command	מִצְוַת לֹא תַעֲשֶׂה	מל״ת
anyway	מִכָּל מָקוֹם	מ״מ
whence these words?	מְנָא הַנֵּי מִילֵּי	מנה״מ
the Master holds	מַר סָבַר	מ״ס
the tractate 'Scribes'	מַסֶּכֶת סוֹפְרִים	
positive command	מִצְוַת עֲשֵׂה	מ״ע
another place	מָקוֹם אַחֵר	מק״א
what is the difference	מַאי שְׁנָא	מ״ש
what he wrote	מַה שֶּׁכָּתַב	
because of this	מִשּׁוּם הָכִי	משו״ה

נ

another version	נוּסְחָא אַחֲרִינָא	נ״א
it appears to me	נִרְאֶה לִי	נ״ל
practical difference	נַפְקָא מִינָהּ	נ״מ

41

ס

book	סֵפֶר	ס'
the help of Heaven	סִייַעְתָּא דִשְׁמַיָא	ס"ד
you might think	סַלְקָא דַעְתָּךְ	
you might think I would say	סַלְקָא דַעְתָּךְ אַמִינָא	סד"א
sign; paragraph	סִימָן	סי'
he holds	סְבִירָא לֵיה	ס"ל

ע

how much more so	עַל אַחַת כַּמָה וְכַמָה	עאכ"ו
on top of	עַל גַּבֵּי	ע"ג
idol worship	עֲבוֹדַת גְּלוּלִים	
peace be upon him!	עָלָיו הַשָׁלוֹם	ע"ה
ignoramus	עַם הָאָרֶץ	
world to come	עוֹלָם הַבָּא	עוה"ב
this world	עוֹלָם הַזֶּה	עוה"ז
idolatry	עֲבוֹדָה זָרָה	ע"ז
thereon	עַל זֶה	
through, by	עַל יְדֵי	ע"י
see	עַיֵין	עי'
thereby	עַל יְדֵי זֶה	עי"ז
see ibid.	עַיֵין שָׁם	עי"ש
therefore	עַל כֵּן	ע"כ
perforce	עַל כָּרְחָךְ	
end of quotation	עַד כָּאן לְשׁוֹנוֹ	עכ"ל
anyway	עַל כָּל פָּנִים	עכ"פ
according to	עַל פִּי	ע"פ

פ

| last chapter | פֶּרֶק בַּתְרָא | פ"ב |

42

second chapter	פֶּרֶק ב׳	פ״ב
first chapter	פֶּרֶק קַמָּא	פ״ק

צ

it should say	צָרִיךְ לוֹמַר	צ״ל
it should be	צָרִיךְ לִהְיוֹת	
this needs great consideration	צָרִיךְ עִיּוּן גָּדוֹל	צע״ג
this needs a little consideration	צָרִיךְ עִיּוּן קְצָת	צע״ק

ק

G-d	קוּדְשָׁא בְּרִיךְ הוּא	קב״ה
argument from minor to major (from the lesser to the greater)	קַל וָחוֹמֶר	ק״ו
we hold	קַיְּמָא לָן	קי״ל
he finds it difficult	קָשֶׁה לֵיהּ	ק״ל
it is easy to understand	קַל לְהָבִין	
it comes to tell us	קָא מַשְׁמַע לָן	קמ״ל
you first thought	קָא סַלְקָא דַעְתָּךְ	קס״ד

ר

Rabbi (title of Tanna, or Amora of Eretz Yisrael)	רַבִּי	ר׳
he means to say	רְצוֹנוֹ לוֹמַר	ר״ל
G-d preserve us!	רַחְמָנָא לִיצְלַן	
initial letters	רָאשֵׁי תֵיבוֹת	ר״ת

ש

bloodshed	שְׁפִיכַת דָּמִים	ש״ד
it is all right	שַׁפִּיר דָּמֵי	

43

learn from it	שְׁמַע מִינָּהּ	ש״מ
the six orders (—the Talmud)	שִׁשָּׁה סְדְרֵי	ש״ס

ת

the inference teaches us	תַּלְמוּד לוֹמַר	ת״ל
let him derive it	תֵּיפּוּק לֵיהּ	
praise be to G-d	תְּהִלָּה לָאֵ־ל	
the first Tanna	תַּנָא קַמָּא	ת״ק
the Rabbis learnt	תָּנוּ רַבָּנָן	ת״ר
come and hear	תָּא שְׁמַע	ת״ש

TALMUDIC ARAMAIC

INTRODUCTION

Aramaic is a language closely related to Hebrew and the basic structure of the two languages is very similar. The following notes will assume in the reader an acquaintance with at least the elements of Hebrew grammar. The Aramaic of the Talmud is clipped and colloquial and differs to some extent in form and style from literary Aramaic. (For the latter the student is referred to the Aramaic portions of the Bible — Daniel ch. 2-7 and Ezra ch. 4-6; and, for a later version of the language, the Targum of Onkelos on the Torah.) These differences will be noted as far as practicable and variations in spelling arising from the unvocalised text of the Talmud will also be pointed out. Talmud students through the ages have created their own brand of "colloquial Aramaic" so far as pronunciation is concerned. The variants have been indicated wherever possible.

NOUNS

Nouns ending in ‎אָ–, הָ–, וֹ–, וִ–, ‎ִי–‎ and ת‎ָ‎–‎ are usually feminine. Other endings are masculine.

The definite article is indicated by the suffix ‎אָ–‎ in the case of masculine nouns, and ‎תָא–‎ (or ‎אֳתָ–‎) in feminine nouns.

The full table of some typical masculine and feminine nouns, including the plural and construct forms, is given below.

MASCULINE NOUNS

Singular	a mouth	פֻּם
Construct	mouth of	־פֻּם
With Def. Art.	the mouth	פּוּמָא
Plural	mouths	פּוּמִין
Construct	mouths of	פּוּמֵי
With Def. Art.	the mouths	פּוּמַיָּא

Singular	a man	גְּבַר
Construct	man of	־גְּבַר
With Def. Art.	the man	גַּבְרָא
Plural	men	גַּבְרִין
Construct	men of	גַּבְרֵי
With Def. Art.	the men	גַּבְרַיָּא

FEMININE NOUNS

Singular	a prayer	צְלוֹ
Construct	prayer of	־צְלוֹת
With Def. Art.	the prayer	צְלוֹתָא
Plural	prayers	צְלָן
Construct	prayers of	־צְלָת
With Def. Art.	the prayers	צְלָוָתָא

Singular	a country	מְדִינָא
Construct	country of	־מְדִינַת
With Def. Art.	the country	מְדִינְתָּא
Plural	countries	מְדִינָן
Construct	countries of	מְדִינָת
With Def. Art.	the countries	מְדִינָתָא

Singular	a camp	מַשְׁרֵי
Construct	camp of	־מַשְׁרֵית
With Def. Art.	the camp	מַשְׁרֵיתָא
Plural	camps	מַשְׁרְיָן
Construct	camps of	מַשְׁרְיָת
With Def. Art.	the camps	מַשְׁרְיָתָא

Singular	an animal	חַיְוָה
Construct	animal of	חֵיוַת־
With Def. Art.	the animal	חֵיוְתָא
Plural	animals	חֵיוָן
Construct	animals of	חֵיוָת־
With Def. Art.	the animals	חֵיוְיָתָא

Note. In the Talmud the final *nun* of the masculine plural is often omitted. Thus:

תְּרֵי גַּבְרֵי two men   הֲנֵי כַּלְבֵּי those dogs

PRONOMINAL SUFFIXES

As in Hebrew, pronominal suffixes play a prominent part in sentence construction. The main ones are as follows:

SINGULAR

Masc. nouns		**Fem. nouns**	
day; the day	יוֹם; יוֹמָא	daughter; the daughter	בְּרַת, בְּרַתָּא
my day	יוֹמִי	my daughter	בְּרַתִּי
your (m s) day	יוֹמָךְ	your daughter	בְּרַתָךְ
his day	יוֹמֵהּ	his daughter	בְּרַתֵּהּ
her day	יוֹמָהּ	her daughter	בְּרַתָּהּ
our day	יוֹמָנָא	our daughter	בְּרַתָנָא
your (m pl) day	יוֹמְכוֹן	your daughter	בְּרַתְכוֹן
their (m) day	יוֹמְהוֹן	their daughter	בְּרַתְהוֹן

PLURAL

animals; the animals	חֵיוָן; חֵיוָיָתָא
my animals	חֵיוָתִי
your (m s) animals	חֵיוָתָךְ
his animals	חֵיוָתֵהּ
her animals	חֵיוָתְהָא

47

our animals	חֵיוָתָנָא
your (m pl) animals	חֵיוָתְכוֹן
their (m) animals	חֵיוָתְהוֹן

fields; the fields	חַקְלִין; חַקְלַיָּא
my fields	חַקְלַי
your (m s) fields	חַקְלָיךְ
his fields	חַקְלוֹהִי
her fields	חַקְלָהָא
our fields	חַקְלָנָא
your (m pl) fields	חַקְלֵיכוֹן
their (m) fields	חַקְלֵיהוֹן

Notes. In the Talmud, which is unvocalised, a ׳ is inserted before the ה in the "his" forms to indicate the pronunciation. Thus שְׁמֵהּ רַבָּא his great name, appears as: שמיה רבא. For a similar reason חַקְלַי appears in the Talmud as חקלאי. Also, the final ן in the "your (pl.)" and "their" forms is usually omitted. Thus: For גְּלִימֵיכוֹן your garments, we have: גלימייכו (usually pronounced גְּלִימַיְכוּ). For חֵיוָתְהוֹן their animal, we have: חיותהו (usually pronounced חֵיוָתְהוּ). Also the form חַקְלוֹהִי his fields, often drops the ה and appears as: חקלוי. (Henceforth in these notes Talmudic variations will be introduced simply by the abbreviation "Talm.")

Syntax. In the Talmud the possessive is generally expressed by use of the preposition דְּ־ of, used as a prefix. Thus: אִילָנֵיא דְחַקְלָא the trees of the field; דִּינָא דִּגְמָרָא the law of tradition.

When the reference is to a particular person or object
the construction is:

בְּרֵהּ דְּרַבִּי אַבָּא   the son of Rabbi Abba (lit. his son, of
Rabbi Abba)

שְׁמַיְיהוּ דְּאִינָשֵׁי people's names (lit. their names, of people).
(This form of the possessive was taken over by Mish-
naic Hebrew. Thus: אִשְׁתּוֹ שֶׁל ר׳ מֵאִיר Rabbi Meir's wife.)

ADJECTIVES

Adjectives agree with the noun and are conjugated
similarly.

שַׁפִּיר beautiful

		Masc. form	Fem. form
Singular	Indefinite	שַׁפִּיר	שַׁפִּירָא
	With def. art.	שַׁפִּירָא	שַׁפִּירְתָּא
Plural	Indefinite	שַׁפִּירִין	שַׁפִּירָן
	With def. art.	שַׁפִּירַיָּא	שַׁפִּירְתָא

Syntax. Noun-adjective syntax is similar to the Hebrew. Examples:

אִתַּת	a woman
אֲרִיכָא	tall (f)
אִתַּת אֲרִיכָא	a tall woman
אִתְּתָא – אֲרִיכָא (הִיא)	the woman is tall
אִתְּתָא אֲרִיכְתָּא	the tall woman
אִילָן	a tree (m)
אָרִיךְ	tall (m)
אִילָן אָרִיךְ	a tall tree
אִילָנָא – אָרִיךְ (הוּא)	the tree is tall
אִילָנָא אֲרִיכָא	the tall tree

Comparatives are expressed by טְפֵי more, and בְּצִיר less; superlatives by: מִכֻּלְהוֹן than all of them.

קָרִיב טְפֵי	nearer	סוּמַק טְפֵי	redder
טַב מִכֻּלְהוֹן	best	טְפֵי מִכֻּלְהוֹן	most

Note also: טוּבָא very; פּוּרְתָּא a little.

קָרִיב טוּבָא	very near	טְפֵי פּוּרְתָּא	a little more

NUMERALS

These are the forms most frequently found:

Cardinal numbers

	M.	F.				
1.	חַד	חֲדָא	11.	חֲדְסַר חַד עֲשַׂר	30.	תְּלָתִין
2.	תְּרֵין / תְּרֵי	תַּרְתֵּי	12.	*תְּרֵיסַר	40.	אַרְבְּעִין
3.	תְּלָתָא	תְּלָת	13.	תְּלֵיסַר	50.	חַמְשִׁין
4.	אַרְבְּעָא	אַרְבַּע	14.	אַרְבֵּיסַר	60.	שִׁתִּין
5.	חַמְשָׁא	חֲמֵשׁ	15.	חֲמֵיסַר	70.	שַׁבְעִין
6.	שִׁתָּא	שִׁית	16.	שִׁיתְּסַר	80.	תְּמַנִין
7.	שַׁבְעָא	שֶׁב	17.	שִׁיבְסַר	90.	תִּשְׁעִין
8.	תְּמַנְיָא	תְּמַנֵּי	18.	תַּמְנֵיסַר	100.	מְאָה
9.	תִּשְׁעָא	תְּשַׁע	19.	תְּשֵׁיסַר	200.	מָאתָן
10.	עַסְרָא	עֲסַר	20.	עֶשְׂרִין	300.	תְּלַת מְאָה

Ordinals

	M.	F.		M.	F.
1st	קַמָּא; קַדְמָאָה קַמָּא, קַדְמָייתָא		6th	שְׁתִיתַאי	שְׁתִיתָאָה
2nd	תִּנְיָן	תִּנְיָינָא, תִּנְיְנָא	7th	שְׁבִיעַאי	שְׁבִיעָאָה
3rd	תְּלִיתַאי	תְּלִיתָאָה	8th	תְּמִינַאי	תְּמִינָאָה
4th	רְבִיעַאי	רְבִיעָאָה	9th	תְּשִׁיעַאי	תְּשִׁיעָאָה
5th	חֲמִישַׁאי	חֲמִישָׁאָה	10th	עֲשִׂירַאי	עֲשִׂירָאָה
			last	בַּתְרָא	בַּתְרָאָה

* Mod. Hebrew: 'a dozen'.

50

Fractions

		Talm.
פַּלְגָּא	a half	
תִּלְתָּא	a third	תילתא
רִבְעָא	a quarter	ריבעא
חֻמְשָׁא	a fifth	חומשא
שְׁתוּת	a sixth	

Proportions

עַל חַד תְּרֵין	two to one
עַל חַד תְּלַת	three to one
חַד מִן עֲשַׂר	one in ten

PRONOUNS

Personal pronouns (which also have the sense of 'I am', 'you are', etc.) are as follows:

I	אֲנָא	we	אֲנַן
you (m & f)	*אַנְתְּ	you (pl)	אַתּוּן
he	אִיהוּ	they	**אִינּוּן
she	אִיהִי		

*Talm. את   **Talm. אינהו, נינהו

Dative

to me	נִיהֲלִי, לִי	to us	לָן, לָנָא
to you	נִיהֲלָךְ, לָךְ	to you	*לְכוֹן
to him	נִיהֲלֵה, לֵה	to them	**לְהוֹן
to her	נִיהֲלָה, לָהּ		

* Talm. לכו   **Talm. להו

Possessive

		Talm.			Talm.
mine	דִּילִי	דידי	ours	דִּילָן	דידן
yours	דִּילָךְ	דידך	yours	דִּילְכוֹן	דידכו
his	דִּילֵה	דידיה	theirs	דִּילְהוֹן	דידהו
hers	דִּילָהּ	דידה			

Syntax. The dative pronouns לֵה and לָהּ are often used in the Talmud to denote the direct object of the verb, while ניהליה is reserved for the indirect object. Thus:

נְסִיב לֵיהּ he took it   אֲמַר לָהּ he said it

51

יְהִיב לֵיהּ וְיהַלְיֵהּ he gave it to him. But לְ ֿ can be **used**
for both; e.g.: מוֹסִיפְנָא לְהוּ לֵיהּ I add them to him (Ḥagiga
5a).

Relative. דִי (or prefix דְ־) stands for: who, which, that.
Interrogative. מַן (Talm. מאן) who? מִי (Talm. מאי)
what? מאן and מאי also stand for: who is? what is?

Demonstrative

This m. דֵין f. הָא, דָא   With def. art.: m. הָדֵין f. הָדָא

That m. הַךְ, הַאי, הַהוּא f. הַהִיא

These הָנְהוּ, הָנַךְ, הַנֵּי Those אִילֵין

Both אִידֵי וְאִידֵי (this one and that one)

Both (f) הָא וְהָא

Syntax

דֵין and דָא follow the noun; הַהוּא and הַהִיא precede it.
שְׁטָרָא הָדֵין this document   הַנֵּי בָּתֵּי those houses
הַהוּא גַּבְרָא that man; a certain man (in an unpleasant
context, also used to refer to oneself.)

PREPOSITIONS

Some of these may be conjugated in a similar way
to the possessive pronouns. E.g.:

From, of, than מִן

	S.	Pl.
1.	מִנִּי	מִנָּן
2.	מִנָּךְ	מִנְכוֹן
3.	מִנֵּיהּ	מִנְהוֹן

Together with בַּהֲדֵי

	S.	Pl.
1.	בַּהֲדִי	בַּהֲדָן
2.	בַּהֲדָךְ	בַּהֲדַיְיכוּ
3.	בַּהֲדֵיהּ	בַּהֲדַיְיהוּ

Within, among	בְּגוֹ		
Note: In Talm. the ו is	1.	בְּגַוִי	בְּגַוָן
doubled, thus בגווי etc.	2.	בְּגַוָךְ	בְּגַוַייכוּ
	3.	בְּגַוֵיה	בְּגַוַייהוּ

Like, as	כְּוַת		
	1.	כְּוָתִי	כְּוָתָן
Note: Talm. כוותי etc.	2.	כְּוָתָךְ	כְּוָתַייכוּ
	3.	כְּוָתֵיה	כְּוָתַייהוּ

Others frequently met with: מִגּוֹ Talm: מיגו out of, from among, following from; לְעֵילָא above לְתַתָּא below.

VERBS

The structure of the Verb in Aramaic follows closely that of the Hebrew.

Each verb-form (or Binyan) is conjugated in the past and future tense and possesses a present participle, imperative and infinitive.

There are six basic Binyanim, of which only the following five occur with any degree of frequency in the Talmud:

Grammatical Name		Corresponding Hebrew Binyan	Function
Pe'al	פְּעַל	קַל	Simple indicative
Itpe'al	אִתְפְּעַל	נִפְעַל	Passive
Pa'al	פַּעֵל	פִּעֵל	Intensive
Af'al	אַפְעֵל	הִפְעִיל	Causative
Itaf'al	אִתַּפְעַל	הִתְפַּעֵל	Reflexive

PE'AL (Simple)

קטר to tie*

* The stem usually employed to illustrate the verb-forms is: קטל to kill. This is however not in accordance with Jewish sensibility and the stem קטר to tie, has been chosen instead.

Past

		Singular		Plural
1.	I tied	קְטַרֵת	we tied	קְטַרְנָא
2. m.	you tied	קְטַרְתְּ	you tied	קְטַרְתּוּן
f.	you tied	קְטַרְתְּ	you tied	קְטַרְתֶּן
3. m.	he tied	קְטַר	they tied	קְטַרוּ
f.	she tied	קְטַרֵת	they tied	קְטַרָא

Talmudic variants:

1st person sing. קְטַרֵת would be spelt קטרית but in practice the ת is often omitted and we find קְטַרֵי I tied; אֲמֵרִי I said, etc.

1st person plural קְטַרְנָא is spelt קטירנא.

3rd person plural קְטַרוּ is spelt קטירו but a colloquial form frequently found in the Talmud omits the י and changes the preceding vowel to וֹ Thus:

אֲמוֹר רַבָּנָן   the Rabbis said

הֲדָר אֲכוֹל   then they ate

כָּל מַאי דְּתִקּוֹן   all that they instituted

Future

		Singular		Plural
1.	I shall tie	אֶקְטַר	we shall tie	נִקְטַר
2. m.	you will tie	תִּקְטַר	you will tie	תִּקְטְרוּן
f.	you will tie	תִּקְטְרִין	you will tie	תִּקְטְרָן
3. m.	he will tie	יִקְטַר	they will tie	יִקְטְרוּן
f.	she will tie	תִּקְטַר	they will tie	תִּקְטְרָן

Talmudic variants:

The forms תִּקְטַר, אֶקְטַר etc. are spelt תקטור, אקטור

Note: For simplicity's sake the feminine plural forms will generally be omitted in the subsequent tables.

Participles

			Singular	Plural
Active	m.	tying	קָטֵר	קָטְרִין
	f.		קָטְרָא	קָטְרָן
Passive	m.	tied	קְטִיר	קְטִירִין
	f.		קְטִירָא	קְטִירָן

Imperative   קְטַר   קְטַרוּ

Infinitive   למיקטר .Talm לְמִקְטַר, מִקְטַר

Standard Variations

As in Hebrew there are standard variations in the conjugation of certain verbs whose root-stems have certain special characteristics. Some examples:

(1) Roots ending in ה־א, ־־, or ־י. E.g. חזא see; בעא ask; שרי begin, הוה be.

The following examples will be conjugated:

חזא to see; הוה to be.

		Past					Future	
Singular	1.		חֲזֵיתִי		הֲוֵיתִי		אֶחֱזֵי	אֱהֱוֵי
	2.	חֲזֵית f	הֲוֵית f		תֶּחֱזֵי	תֶּהֱוֵי
	3.	חֲזָת חֲזָא	הֲוָת הֲוָה		יֶחֱזֵי	יֶהֱוֵי
Plural	1.		חֲזֵינָא		הֲוֵינָא		נֶחֱזֵי	נֶהֱוֵי
	2.		חֲזֵיתוּן		הֲוֵיתוּן		תֶּחֱזוּן	תֶּהֱווּן
	3.		חֲזוֹ		הֲווֹ		יֶחֱזוּן	יֶהֱווּן

Participles

		Active			Passive	
		f		f		f
s.	חֲזֵי חַזַת	הֲוֵי הֲוַת	חֲזֵי* חַזְיָא
pl.	חָזֵין	הָוֵין	חַזְיָן

(*usu. pron. חֲזִי)

	Imperative			Infinitive	
s.	חֲזִי	הֲוִי	(לְ)מֶחֱזֵי (לְ)מֶהֱוֵי
pl.	חֲזוּ	הֲווּ	

(2)　Verbs whose roots begin with א change the א
into י in the Future. Thus: אתא to come.

Singular 1.　אֵיתֵי　I shall come

2.　תֵּיתֵי　you will come

3.　יֵיתֵי　he will come　תֵּיתֵי she will come

Plural　1.　נֵיתֵי　we will come

2.　תֵּיתוּן　you will come

3.　יֵיתוּן　they will come

(3)　Roots with ו or י as 2nd letter. E.g. קוּם rise;
שִׂים place, put.

Example: קוּם to rise

		Past	Future
Singular	1.	קָמִית	אֵקוּם
	2.	קָמְתְּ	תְּקוּם
	3.	קָם, קָאם	יְקוּם
Plural	1.	קָמְנָא	נְקוּם
	2.	קָמְתּוּן	תְּקוּמוּן
	3.	קָמוּ	יְקוּמוּן

Participle
Active קָאֵם Talm. קָאִים abbr. קָאִי

Imperative	s.	pl.	Infinitive
	קוּם	קוּמוּ	(לְ)מֵיקַם

(4) Roots whose first letter is נ drop the נ
in the future tense. Example: נפק to go out.

		Future			
Sing.	1.	אֶפֵּק	Pl.	1.	נִפֵּק
	2.	תִּפֵּק		2.	תִּפְּקוּן
	3.	יִפֵּק		3.	יִפְּקוּן

SYNTAX

(1) In the colloquial Aramaic of the Talmud a great
deal of use is made of the present participle, in
conjunction with personal pronouns as suffixes.

E.g.:

סָלֵק אֲנָא) סָלְקְנָא)	I go up (usu. pron. סָלִיקְנָא)
סָלֵק אַתְּ) סָלְקַתְּ)	you go up
סָלְקִין אֲנַן) סָלְקִינַן)	we go up (usu. pron. סָלְקִינָן)

Similarly: בָּעֵי wanting, asking; בָּעֵינָא I want; בָּעֵינַן
we want; אָמֵר saying; אָמְרְנָא (contr. אמינא)
usu. pron. אַמִינָא) I say; אָמְרִינַן we say (contr.
אמינן).

(2) The past of "to be" with the participle is often
used to express continuous action in the past.
E.g.: הֲוָה אָמֵר he used to say
Similarly the future of "to be" with the participle
expresses continuous action in the future. E.g.
יְהוֹן נָסְבִין they will be taking.
The 3rd person past tense of "to be" is also
used with the participle to express the sub-
junctive mood. E.g.

הֲוָה אֲמֵינָא I would have said; I might have said.
הֲוָה לָן לְמֵיזַל we should have gone (lit. it was for us to go).

(3) The particle קָא often precedes the past tense
or present participles of verbs with emphatic
effect. It is derived from the participle קָאֵי, קָאֵים
standing, stands; i.e. the action described
"stands", is confirmed. (Cf. the use of the auxil-
iary verb "to do" in "he **did** go".) It is often con-
tracted to קָ and used as a prefix. E.g.

קָאָתֵינָא, קָא אָתֵינָא	I come (usu. pron. קָאָתֵינָא)
קָאָמֵר, קָא אָמֵר	he says (usu. pron. קָאָמֵר)
קָתָנֵי, קָא תָּנֵי	he learns

57

(4) The prefix לְ- (or לִ-) prefixed to the 3rd person future of many verbs has the sense
of "let one", "let him". It appears to be a contraction of the infinitive: לִיגְמַר – לְמִיגְמַר

E.g. יֵיתֵי he will come; לְמֵיתֵי to come; לֵיתֵי let him come
יִגְרַס he will read; לְמִיגְרַס to read; לִיגְרַס let him read

לִיגְמַר אִינַשׁ בְּרֵישָׁא וַהֲדַר לִיסַבַּר

one should learn first and only then analyse

(5) The passive participle of חזא to see —
חֲזֵי (m), חַזְיָא (f) — appears very often in the
sense of "fit, fitting" (as Heb. רָאוּי).
(Cf. "visa" in diplomatic usage.)

OTHER BINYANIM

We give below the conjugation tables of the other
four verb-forms met with in the Talmudic literature.
(Feminine endings omitted for simplicity.)

	אִתְּפְעַל Passive was tied	פַּעֵל Intensive tied up	אַפְעֵל Causative caused to tie	אִתְפְּעַל Reflexive tied myself
Past				
Sing. 1.	אִתְקְטַרֵת	קַטְּרֵת	אַקְטְרֵת	אִתְקַטְּרֵת
2.	אִתְקְטַרְתְּ	קַטֵּרְתְּ	אַקְטַרְתְּ	אִתְקַטַּרְתְּ
3.	אִתְקְטַר	קַטַּר	אַקְטַר	אִתְקַטַּר
Plur. 1.	אִתְקְטַרְנָא	קַטַּרְנָא	אַקְטַרְנָא	אִתְקַטַּרְנָא
2.	אִתְקְטַרְתּוּן	קַטַּרְתּוּן	אַקְטַרְתּוּן	אִתְקַטַּרְתּוּן
3.	אִתְקְטַרוּ	קַטִּירוּ	אַקְטַרוּ	אִתְקַטַּרוּ
Future	will be tied	will tie up	will cause to tie	will tie (my)self
Sing. 1.	אֶתְקְטַר	אֲקַטֵּר	אַקְטֵר	אֶתְקַטַּר
2.	תִּתְקְטַר	תְּקַטֵּר	תַּקְטֵר	תִּתְקַטַּר
3.	יִתְקְטַר	יְקַטֵּר	יַקְטֵר	יִתְקַטַּר
Plur. 1.	נִתְקְטַר	נְקַטֵּר	נַקְטֵר	נִתְקַטַּר
2.	תִּתְקַטְרוּן	תְּקַטְּרוּן	תְּקַטְרוּן	תִּתְקַטְּרוּן
3.	יִתְקַטְרוּן	יְקַטְּרוּן	יַקְטְרוּן	יִתְקַטְּרוּן

Participle	being tied	tying up	causing to tie	tying oneself
	מִתְקְטַר	מְקַטֵּר	מַקְטַר	מִתְקַטַּר
Infinitive	to be tied	to tie up	to cause to tie	to tie oneself
	אִתְקְטָרָא	קַטָּרָא	אַקְטָרָא	אִתְקַטָּרָא

Standard Variations

Some variations occur in the above forms, related to the occurrence of certain letters in the root-stems, as outlined above in the case of the Pe'al. It has not been thought necessary to list these here in full; they can be deduced in most cases without much difficulty from the notes given previously. Some special cases are given below.

(1) Verbs whose roots commence with א change the א to י in the Af'al. Roots ending in ה, א or י undergo the variations mentioned above for the Pe'al. The verb אתא "to come" combines both these characteristics, and is conjugated in the Af'al as follows:

אתא to come   Af'al אַיְתָא to make come, to bring

		Past		**Future**	
			Talm.		Talm.
Sing.	1.	אַיְתֵית	אייתית	אַיְיתֵי	אייתי
	2.	אַיְתֵית	אייתית	תַּיְתֵי	תייתי
	3.	אַיְתֵי	אייתי	יַיְתֵי	
Plur.	1.	אַיְתֵינָא	אייתינא	נַיְתֵי	נייתי
	2.	אַיְתֵיתוּן	אייתיתון	תַּיְתוּן	תייתו
	3.	אַיְתֵיוּ	אייתיו	יַיְתוּן	ייתו
Participle		מַיְתֵי	מייתי		
Infinitive		אַיְתָא	אייתא		

59

(2) Ithpe'al (passive). In some verbs whose 1st root-
letter is a sibilant or dental, the ת of the Ithpe'al
comes after this first root-letter (as in Hebrew
in the Hitpa'el

Thus: סַיֵם to note; תִּסְתַּיֵם let it be noted.

שמע to hear; מִשְׁתְּמַע it is heard; implied

Where the first root-letter is ז, the ת is replaced
by ד inserted between the 1st and 2nd letter of
the root.

זַבַּן he sold; מִזְדַּבַּן it is sold.

Where the first letter is ת the ת of the Ithpe'al
is elided: תְּבַר he broke; אִתְּבַר it was broken.

In Talmudic Aramaic the ת of the Ithpe'al is
often omitted in other verbs. E.g.

מִתְבְּעֵי – מִיבְּעֵי	it is needed
מִתְקְטֵל – מִיקְטֵל	he gets killed
מִתְחַסְּרָא – מֵיחַסְרָא	it is lacking
אִתְקְלַע – אִיקְלַע	he visited
מִתְמַנְּעֵי – מִימְנְעֵי	they are prevented
אִתְקַרְיָא – אִיקַרְיָא	she was called
אִתְחֲזִי – אִיחֲזִי	had become fit

SYNTAX

(1) In Aramaic the verb generally comes at the end
of the sentence. Thus:

בֵּאדַיִן דָּנִיֵּאל לְמַלְכָּא אֲזַל lit. Then Daniel to the king went.
But in the Talmud this rule is not always
adhered to.

(2) The function of the Binyanim may be found to
vary. Words which have a simple sense in English may be conjugated in the Af'al in Aramaic.
Thus "he found" is אַשְׁכַּח an Af'al form. The same
may apply to the Pa'al (intensive); e.g. "he

praised" is שַׁבַּח a Pa'al form. Note also: זְבַן
he bought; זַבֵּן (Pa'al) he sold. גְּמַר he learnt;
אַגְמַר (Af'al) he taught.

(3) The infinitive is sometimes used in conjunction
with the active verb for emphasis (as in Biblical,
but not Mishnaic, Hebrew). Thus:

מִיגְנַב גְּנָבִי מִינֵּיהּ they stole it from him (lit. perhaps:

"as far as stealing is concerned, they stole it");

מִקְרַע לָא תִּקְרְעוּהוּ וּמִיגְמַר נַמֵּי לָא תִּגְמְרוּ מִנַּיהּ

you should not tear it up but you should also not
learn from it (Bava Bathra 130b).

(4) The passive participle is often used in conjunction
with לִי or לֵיהּ to express a state of affairs.

לָא שְׁמִיעָא לִי it is not heard by me (I have not heard it)
סְבִירָא לֵיהּ it is held by him (he holds it—i.e. an opinion).

PRONOMINAL SUFFIXES

These are much used in simple sentences when
the object of the verb is: me, you, him, etc. They are
given below for verbs in the Pe'al or simple form, but
can be used with any active Binyan.

Object	קְטַרִת I tied	קְטַרְתְּ you tied	קְטַר he tied	קְטַרְנָא we **tied**	קְטַרְתּוּן you tied	קְטַרוּ they tied
me	—	קְטַרְתָּן	קַטְרָן	—	קְטַרְתּוּנִי	קְטַרוּנִי
you (s.)	קְטַרְתָּךְ	—	קַטְרָךְ	קְטַרְנָךְ	—	קְטַרוּךְ
him	קְטַרְתֵּיהּ	קְטַרְתֵּיהּ	קַטְרֵיהּ	קְטַרְנֵיהּ	קְטַרְתּוּנֵהּ	קְטַרוּהִי
her	קְטַרְתָּהּ	קְטַרְתָּהּ	קַטְרָהּ	קְטַרְנָהּ	קְטַרְתּוּנָהּ	קְטַרוּהָ
us	—	קְטַרְתָּנָא	קַטְרָנָא	—	קְטַרְתּוּנָא	קְטַרוּנָא

61

	I tied	you tied	he tied	we tied	you tied	they tied
you (pl.)	קְטַרְתְּכוֹן	–	קְטַרְכוֹן	קְטַרְנְכוֹן	–	קְטַרוּכוֹן
them	קְטַרְתִּינְהוּ	קְטַרִינְהוּ	קְטַרְתִּינְהוּ	קְטַרִינִינְהוּ	קְטַרְתּוּנוֹן	קְטַרוּנוֹן

SYNTAX

The pronominal suffix is usually attached to the verb even though the object is expressly referred to in the sentence. Thus: אֲנָא תוֹרִי בְּבֵירָךְ אַשְׁכְּחִיתֵּיה
I found my ox in your pit (lit.: I, my ox, in your pit I found it).

בְּעָא מִנֵּיה רַב פָּפָּא מֵאַבַּיֵי   R. Papa asked of him: of Abaye

HEBREW-ARAMAIC ROOT-LETTER CORRESPONDENCES

It can be helpful in identifying Aramaic words if one knows that certain Hebrew consonants are replaced by different consonants in Aramaic in a more or less standard way. These correspondences are by no means invariable but they occur with sufficient frequency to be useful. Some examples:

Heb.	Ar.	Trans.	Heb.	Ar.	Trans.
שׁ	ת		צ	ע	
שָׁלֹשׁ	תְּלַת	three	רֹבֵץ	רְבַע	lie down
שֶׁלֶג	תְּלַג	snow	עֵץ	אָע	wood
שַׁעַר	תַּרְעָא	gate	אֶרֶץ	אַרְעָא	land
שׁוֹר	תּוֹר	ox	רָצוֹן	רַעֲוָא	goodwill
צ	ט		ז	ד	
עֵצָה	עֵיטָא	advice	זָכָר	דְּכַר	male
עֶצֶם	אַטְמָא	bone	זֶה, זֹאת	דֵּן, דָּא	this
צֵל	טוּלָא	shade	אֹזֶן	אוּדְנָא	ear
רוּץ	רְהַט	run	זָב	דָּאֵיב	flow

END-PIECE

A few notes on Hebrew vocalisation

(1) Accuracy in vocalisation and pronunciation is often essential to clarity of thought. Even a misplaced accent can lead to a complete change of meaning. E.g.:

בָּ֫נוּ in us בָּנ֫וּ they built (root בנה);

שָׁ֫בוּ they returned (root שוב);

שָׁב֫וּ they captured (root שבה);

שָׁ֫תוּ they placed (root שות);

שָׁת֫וּ they drank (root שתה).

(2) The Hiphil of ע״ו verbs sometimes gives rise to some confusion in vocalisation. These are the correct forms:

Root	Past	Present	Future	Infinitive
שוב	הֵשִׁיב	מֵשִׁיב	יָשִׁיב	לְהָשִׁיב
בוא	הֵבִיא	מֵבִיא	יָבִיא	לְהָבִיא
עוד	הֵעִיד	מֵעִיד	יָעִיד	לְהָעִיד
זוד	הֵזִיד	מֵזִיד	יָזִיד	לְהָזִיד
סור	הֵסִיר	מֵסִיר	יָסִיר	לְהָסִיר
רום	הֵרִים	מֵרִים	יָרִים	לְהָרִים

(3) The correct form of pronominal suffixes should also be noted. They must often be distinguished from the simple past tense of verbs, and from the gerund form (much used in Biblical Hebrew). Thus:

Simple past	Past with pronom. suffix	Gerund with pronom. suffix
שָׁמְרוּ	שְׁמָרוֹ	שָׁמְרוֹ
they guarded	he guarded him	his guarding
שָׁמְרָה	שְׁמָרָה	שָׁמְרָה
she guarded	he guarded her	her guarding

It is clear that failure to distinguish נָתְנָה לוֹ 'she gave to him' from נְתָנָהּ לוֹ 'he gave her/it to him' can easily lead to confusion.

MEMORY AID

which?	הֵי	this	הָא
where?	הֵיכָא	here	הָכָא
how?	הֵיכִי	so	הָכִי

APPENDIX 1

INTRODUCTION TO THE TALMUD
by
RABBI SAMUEL HA-NAGID[1]

In which he records everything that a beginner needs to know to ease his path in the study of the Talmud.

1. The Talmud is divided into two parts: (a) the Mishna; and (b) the commentary on the Mishna.

2. The Mishna is what is called the "Oral Law". It contains the essential Torah transmitted orally from Moshe Rabbenu to the time of Rabbi Judah the Holy, also known as Rabbi Judah the Prince [ca. 130-220 C.E.], who committed it to writing to ensure its long-term survival in face of the danger that it might be forgotten and lost. [The Mishna also includes much rabbinic legislation promulgated by the Rabbis to safeguard the Torah, in the form of סְיָגִים, גְּזֵירוֹת וְתַקָּנוֹת "fences", decrees and ordinances.]

---

[1] "Nagid" (=Prince, Ruler) was the title given to the acknowledged head of the Jewish community in Moslem Spain, and also in Egypt. It used to be assumed that the "Rabbi Samuel Ha-Nagid" mentioned here was the distinguished bearer of this name who flourished in Spain in the 11th century and who was a famous talmudist, philosopher, poet and statesman (993-1060). There is however clear evidence that the actual author of this Introduction was another Rabbi Samuel Ha-Nagid who was head of the Egyptian Jewish community about the middle of the 12th Century.

It seems to have been written for adult students who were commencing the study of the Talmud and needed a guide to its structure and methodology. The brief survey it gives can be of great benefit to those of us who find ourselves today in a very similar situation.

This translation is based on a manuscript version in the Sassoon collection (No. 1046), and thanks are given to my friend

3. This work can also be divided into two parts: (a) established law; and (b) rejected law. The established law [insofar as it refers to legislation contained in the Torah itself — *min ha-Torah*] is that which was learned direct from Moshe Rabbenu, who received it direct from the Almighty. It may appear in the name of a single sage or in the name of many, as will be explained later.

4. "Rejected law" is that side of a dispute which though recorded has not been accepted. This may also appear in the name of a single sage or of many. The question may be asked: Why did Rabbenu Ha-Kadosh (Rabbi Judah the Holy) record those matters which are not accepted as law? Surely it would have been better to include only such laws as are binding? The answer is that during the early times each sage recorded for himself all that he had learned, whether accepted or not. When Rabbenu Ha-Kadosh came to record the Mishna he felt compelled to include those views which were not accepted, so as to avoid the possibility of someone bringing forward these opinions, which he may have heard from one of the sages, and endeavouring to contradict the accepted law. If he did so, he could easily be refuted by pointing out that they represent views that have not been accepted. This is pointed out by the Sages in the Mishna [*Eduyot,* chap. 1], where they say: "Why were the words of the single sage

Rabbi S.D. Sassoon and to the Institute of Microfilmed Hebrew Manuscripts of the Jewish National & University Library of Jerusalem for their permission to use the microfilm of this manuscript (No. 9291).

The introductory sentence printed in bold type appears only in the manuscript version. Sentences found in the printed editions and not in the manuscript, when included, have been enclosed in braces { }. The numbering of the paragraphs and sub-paragraphs and some items of additional information and clarification have been supplied by the translator. The latter are given in square brackets. The printed version may be found in the Vilna Shass, where it appears after *Massecheth Berachoth.*

recorded beside the words of the majority to no apparent purpose? Because if anyone were to come and say, 'I heard such-and-such', they will be able to tell him 'You heard this from so-and-so'; meaning 'and this is not the law.'" [2]

5. Thus far we have been discussing the first part of the Talmud, which is the Mishna. The second part, which is the commentary on the Mishna, is called the Gemara [i.e., tradition]. This comprises many components, twenty-one in all; such as Tosefta, Beraitha, explanations, questions, answers, difficulties and their solutions, and many others, which will now be briefly explained.

[1] *Tosefta* ("Addition") is a form of Beraitha — mishnaic material not included in the Mishna — [and is appended to every tractate of the Mishna]. In the Talmud it is usually introduced by the word תַּנְיָא. When it follows the rulings of the Mishna it is accepted as law. [It contains much valuable information, throwing light on many a mishna.]

[2] *Beraitha* ("outside material") includes all the other mishnaic material compiled and transmitted by sages after the Mishna, such as the mishnaic material compiled

---

[2]Note on the origin of disputes (from Maimonides' Introduction to his Commentary to the Mishna):

"Disputes arose only in those parts of the law derived by reasoning. They occurred in connection with matters of fine detail on which no ruling had been transmitted and which consequently had to be derived by a process of deduction and analogy, on the basis of principles and rulings previously handed down. Now it is well known that no two sages think exactly alike, and so disputes arose as to what principle to apply to the precise point of detail under discussion and how to apply it. Particularly in later generations, when troubles and persecutions affected the intensity of learning and the clarity of the thinking process, disputes in matters of detail became quite frequent, and are recorded in the Mishna, and the law is decided according to the majority opinion, or in accordance with rules laid down."

and recorded by Rabbi Ḥiyya [favourite disciple of Rabbi Judah the Prince] and Rabbi Oshaya; the *Mishna* of Rabbi Eliezer b. Yaakov, the *Mechilta* of Rabbi Yishmael, the Letters of Rabbi Akiva; as well as the legal midrashim which follow verses of the Torah, such as *Mechilta* on Exodus, *Torat Kohanim* (or *Sifra*) on Leviticus and *Sifre* on Numbers and Deuteronomy. These are generally introduced by the words תָּנוּ רַבָּנָן and conflicting statements by the words תָּנֵי חֲדָא...תַּנְיָא אִידָךְ. All Beraitha material which is not contested in the Gemara is accepted as law; where there is a dispute the law is decided according to the rulings given [see paragraphs [6], [7], [8] below].

[3] *Peyrush* (explanation) is the elucidation by the Gemara of matters contained in the Mishna, and is marked by the words "What is so-and-so?" followed by the explanation.

[4] *She'eyla* (Aramaic: בָּעְיָא) is a request for a ruling, and may be addressed by one group to another (אַבַּעְיָא לְהוּ), or by a group to an individual (בְּעוּ מִינֵיהּ), or by one individual to another (בְּעָא מִינֵיהּ). The law is determined by the replies given.

[5] *Teshuva* is the answer given to the enquiries mentioned above, and it is established as law in accordance with the rulings given.

[6] *Difficulty* (Aramaic: קוּשְׁיָא) refers to an objection raised against the opinion of an Amora by citation of an [apparently] conflicting source. . . . If raised by more than one sage it is introduced by מֵתִיבֵי and if by one: אֵיתִיבֵיה.

[7] *Resolution* (Aramaic: פֵּירוּקָא) is the answer given resolving the difficulty and if not disputed is [often] accepted as law. [See also [18] below.]

[8] *Refutation* (תִּיּוּבְתָּא) occurs where a ruling is refuted by clear proofs; the law is then decided according to the strength of the proofs. [If the statement of an Amora — a sage of the Talmud — is found to be contradicted by a Tanna — a sage of the Mishna — he is thereby refuted, unless he can find another Tanna to support him.]

[9] *Support* (Aramaic: סְיַיעְתָּא) is a source cited to strengthen a given ruling and to support its acceptance; introduced by the words לֵימָא מְסַיַּע לֵיהּ.

[10] *Contradiction* (רוּמְיָא) occurs when an apparent contradiction between two [equivalent] sources is pointed out. Introduced by רָבִּי...רָמֵי , וּרְמִינְהִי , וּרְמִינהוּ.

[11] *Necessity* (צְרִיכוּתָא): a demonstration that each of two or more apparently similar statements in a source is needed, [because each contains some information not provided by the other(s)]. Introduced by וּצְרִיכָא .

[12] *Attack* (אַתְקַפְתָּא) is an objection raised [on the basis of reasoning rather than the citation of conflicting sources]. It is found only in connection with Amoraim (the sages of the later, Gemara, period) and is introduced by מַתְקִיף לָהּ רַבִּי... . The decision is as in [8] above.

[13] *Case* (Heb. מַעֲשֶׂה; Aramaic: עוּבְדָּא) is the citation of an actual happening on which a decision is reported.

[14] *Tradition* (Aramaic: שְׁמַעְתְּתָא) is a saying containing information on a halachic subject. Opposite: Aggada [see [19] below.]

[15] *Sugya* (סוּגְיָא) is a connected passage of Gemara containing a series of questions and answers.

[16] *Hilchetha* (הִילְכְתָא): a decision rendered in a case of dispute, where the Gemara concludes "The halacha is according to so-and-so."

[17] *Teyku* (תֵּיקוּ)[literally: "let it stand"] occurs where there is a doubt in the Gemara on a point of halacha and the matter is left without decision. If it relates to a money matter the practice is to follow the lenient ruling [i.e., the defendant is exempted from payment]; and in the case of prohibitions, the practice is to follow the more stringent ruling [except in the case of some rabbinic prohibitions]. . . .

[18] *Interpretation* (Aramaic: שִׁינוּיָא): where a sage is faced with a contradiction from an accepted source and he endeavours to re-interpret the source so that it no longer conflicts with his view. . . .

[19] *Aggada* (Aramaic: אֲגַדְתָּא): everything mentioned in the Gemara which is not directly connected with the halachic aspect of a commandment. One should learn from such statements only those things which our minds can grasp. It is important to know that all matters which our Sages established as law, in connection with a commandment transmitted by Moshe Rabbenu who received it from the Almighty, cannot be augmented or diminished in any way. However, the [aggadic] explanations they rendered of biblical verses were in accordance with their individual views and the ideas which occurred to them. We should learn from them insofar as our minds can grasp them; but otherwise we should not build upon them. [Since we have not succeeded in understanding the deeper meaning of their words, we should not attempt to use them as the basis of our thinking.]

[20] *Teaching* (Heb. הוֹרָאָה) is a tradition regarding a commandment issuing from the sages in assemblies or academies.

[21] *Shitta* (Heb. שִׁיטָה) refers to a number of individual sages each reported as holding a similar opinion and cited together as such in the Gemara; in which case we are told that the decision is not like any of them. {You should know that the Talmud was completed in the time of Ravina and Rav Ashi [5th C.] and it is they who taught us the secrets of its compilation, including such rules as the above.}

6. The rules for arriving at decisions in disputes between Tannaim [sages of the Mishna] are as follows:

[1] One against many: the halacha (final decision) is like the many.

[2] A dispute in one mishna followed by an anonymous statement [representing one of the views] in another mishna means that the halacha is in accordance with the latter. [This applies only within one tractate].

[3] An anonymous mishna followed by a mishna containing a dispute on the same point means that the halacha is not like the anonymous mishna. [This also applies only within one tractate.]

[4] If there is a dispute in a *beraitha* and an anonymous statement in a mishna [following one view], the halacha is like the latter.

[5] If there is a dispute in a mishna and an anonymous statement in a *beraitha*, we do not say the halacha is like the *beraitha*, because we say "If Rabbi [Judah the Prince] did not teach it, how could Rabbi Ḥiyya [the editor of the Beraitha] know it?"

7. Further rules relating to Mishna and Beraitha:

[1] An anonymous mishna is according to Rabbi Meir.

[2] An anonymous statement in the Tosefta is according to Rabbi Neḥemia.

[3] An anonymous statement in *Sifra* is like Rabbi Yehuda;

[4] and in *Sifre*, like Rabbi Shimon; and all of them are in general agreement with Rabbi Akiva, whose disciples they were.

[5] Where Rabbi Meir is named in a source, and his decision is disputed, either by Rabbi Yehuda, Rabbi Yose, Rabbi Shimon or Rabbi Eliezer ben Yaakov, the halacha is like his opponent.

[6] Rabbi Yehuda against Rabbi Shimon: the halacha is like Rabbi Yehuda.

[7] [The halacha is always like Rabbi Yose, even against more than one Tanna.]

[8] The *Mishna* of Rabbi Eliezer ben Yaakov is "small but pure" [i.e., he is not mentioned often, but when he is the halacha is always like him].

[9] "Some say" (יֵשׁ אוֹמְרִים) means Rabbi Nathan.

[10] "Others say" (אֲחֵרִים אוֹמְרִים) means Rabbi Meir.

[11] Wherever Rabban Shimon ben Gamliel appears in our Mishna the halacha is like him, except in three (named) cases. . . .

[12] The halacha is always like Rabbi [Judah the Prince] where he disputes with one other sage. . . .

[13] However, wherever Rabbi [Judah the Prince] disputes with his father [Rabban Shimon ben Gamliel] the halacha is like his father.

[14] Wherever a mishna is cited in the name of Rabbi Shimon ben Elazar and there is no dispute mentioned, the halacha is like him.

[15] Rabbi Eliezer against Rabban Gamliel: the halacha is like Rabban Gamliel. . . .

[16] [The halacha is always like Rabbi Akiva when in dispute with one other sage.]

[17] Beth Shammai against Beth Hillel — the halacha is like Beth Hillel, except in six cases, where the Sages said the decision is like neither of them, and three cases where the halacha is like Beth Shammai.

[18] Whenever a Tanna qualifies his remarks by stating "in which case does this apply" בַּמֶּה דְבָרִים אֲמוּרִים or "When does this apply? In such-and-such circumstances", the halacha is like him. Similarly, a mishna introduced by the words "In truth they said" בֶּאֱמֶת אָמְרוּ represents the undisputed halacha.

[19] We do not learn the halacha from a mishna alone, but only from the decision given in the Talmud.

8. These are the rules relating to disputes between Amoraim (the sages of the Talmud):

[1] Rav against Shmuel — the halacha is like Rav in prohibitions and like Shmuel in civil laws. [Rav is Rav Abba Aricha (the Tall), 3rd C. The title 'Rav' is given to Amoraim of Babylon. Amoraim of Eretz Yisrael, like Tannaim, are all called 'Rabbi'.]

[2] Rav Hisda against Rav Huna: the halacha is like Rav Huna.

[3] Rav Sheshet against Rav Nahman — the halacha is like Rav Sheshet in prohibitions and like Rav Nahman in civil laws.

[4] The halacha is never like the disciple when in dispute with his teacher.

[5] If a later sage is in dispute with an earlier sage, the halacha is like the later sage. [Since both are within one era — the era of the Amoraim — and therefore of equal status, the opinion of the later one prevails, since he has had the opportunity of considering all the developments of the argument that have taken place in the interim period.]

[6] Rav Yehuda against Rabbah: the halacha is like Rav Yehuda.

[7] Rabbah against Rav Yosef: the halacha is like Rabbah, except in three (named) cases.

[8] Rav Aḥa against Ravina: the halacha is like Ravina, except in three (named) cases.

[9] The compilers of the Talmud were Rav Ashi and Ravina and their colleagues [5th C.]; and in their time the Talmud was completed.

[10] The halacha is like Mar the son of Rav Ashi except where he is in dispute with his teacher. . . .

[11] Wherever the Gemara says, "So-and-so is refuted" [see 4 [8], above] the halacha is not like that sage. [However, where the Gemara concludes merely with the word *kashya* ("this is difficult") this indicates that the difficulty is merely textual and can be resolved.]

[12] Any dispute which is merely theoretical and has no practical relevance does not have the words "the halacha is like so-and-so" applied to it.

APPENDIX 2

TALMUDIC WEIGHTS AND MEASURES

1. LINEAR

PARSAH פַּרְסָה (Based on Persian parasang)	MIL מִיל (approximately 1 kilometer)	AMMAH אַמָּה (Arm's length)	ZERET זֶרֶת (Span)	TEFACH טֶפַח (Hands-breadth)	ETZBA' אֶצְבַּע (Thumb-width)	APPROXIMATE MODERN EQUIVALENTS	
						American	Metric
1	4	8,000	16,000	48,000	192,000	2.68 mi.	4320 m.
	1	2,000	4,000	12,000	48,000	1180 yds.	1080 m.
		1	2	6	24	21.25 in.	54 cm.
			1	3	12	10.6 in.	27 cm.
				1	4	3.5 in.	9 cm.
					1	0.9 in.	2.25 cm.

Note: The "approximate modern equivalents" given here are based on the findings of Rabbi Moshe Feinstein *sh'lita*. Some authorities reduce this estimate by about 10% (Rabbi A. H. Noeh *zatzal*); while others increase it by about 10% (Chazon Ish *zatzal*).

74

2. CAPACITY

SOLID	EPHAH איפה	SE'AH סאה	TARKAV תרקב	OMER עומר	KAV קב	ROVA' רבע	LOG לג	REVI'IT רביעית	BEYTSAH ביצה	KEZAYIT כזית	APPROXIMATE MODERN EQUIVALENTS American	Metric
LIQUID	BAT בת		HIN הין									
											gallons	*litres*
	1	3	6	10	18	72	72	288	432	864	6.5	24.8
		1	2	3⅓	6	24	24	96	144	288	2.2	8.3
			1	1⅔	3	12	12	48	72	144	1.1	4.1
				1	1.8	7.2	7.2	28.8	43.2	86.4	*pints* 5.2	2.5
					1	4	4	16	24	48	2.9	1.4
						1	1	4	6	12	0.7	0.3
								1	1½	3	*fluid oz.* 2.9	*cu. cm.* 86
									1	2	1.9	57
										1	0.9	28

Note: The "approximate modern equivalents" given here are based on the findings of Rabbi A. H. Noeh zatzal. For the purposes of certain mitzvot the equivalents given here are increased by over 50% (*Mishna Brura, Biur Halacha,* 271:13, and Rabbi Moshe Feinstein sh'lita) or by 75% (Chazon Ish zatzal).

3. GRAIN MEASURES

KOR כֹּר	LETECH לֶתֶךְ	SE'AH סְאָה	KAV קַב	ROVA' רֹבַע	APPROXIMATE MODERN EQUIVALENTS	
					American	Metric
					bushels	*litres*
1	2	30	180	720	7.0	246.2
	1	15	90	360	3.5	123.1
					gallons	
		1	6	24	1.9	8.2
					pints	
			1	4	2.5	1.4
				1	0.6	0.3

See note to Table 2.

4. AREA

name of area	i.e. the area in which the amount of grain that can be sown is:	equivalent in square *ammot*	APPROXIMATE MODERN EQUIVALENTS	
			American *acres*	Metric *hectares*
בֵּית כּוֹר BET KOR	1 KOR	75,000	4.37	1.77
בֵּית סָאתַיִם BET SA'ATAYIM	2 SE'AH	5,000	1409 *sq. yards*	1178 *sq. meters*
בֵּית סְאָה BET SE'AH	1 SE'AH	2,500	705	589
בֵּית קַב BET KAV	1 KAV	416 $\frac{2}{3}$	117	98
בֵּית רֹבַע BET ROVA'	1 ROVA'	104 $\frac{1}{6}$	29	24

5. WEIGHT

KIKAR כִּכָּר	MANEH* מָנֶה	PRASS פְּרָס	SELA‘** סֶלַע	DINAR דִּינָר	APPROXIMATE MODERN EQUIVALENTS	
					American	Metric
					pounds	*kilograms*
1	60	120	1500	6000	56.2	25.5
						grams
	1	2	25	100	1.0	425.0
		1	12½	50	0.5	212.5
					ounces	
			1	4	0.6	17.0
				1	0.15	4.25

*Also referred to as *litra* לִיטְרָא = approximately 1 pound.
**Talmudic term for the Biblical *shekel*.

6. COINAGE

MANEH מָנֶה	SELA' * סֶלַע	DINAR (ZUZ) דִּינָר (זוּז)	MA'AH מָעָה	PUNDION פּוּנְדְּיוֹן	ISSAR אִסָּר	PERUTAH פְּרוּטָה
	S I L V E R			C O P P E R		
1	25	100	600	1200	2400	19,200
	1	4	24	48	96	768
		1	6	12	24	192
			1	2	4	32
				1	2	16
					1	8

1 GOLDEN DINAR דִּינָר זָהָב = 25 SILVER DINARIM כֶּסֶף דִּינְרֵי

---

*Talmudical term for the Biblical *shekel*; but the term "shekel" is sometimes colloquially used to denote a half-*sela'*.

Some examples of purchasing power in the time of the Mishna:

A laborer's daily wage could amount to 4 *zuz* (=*dinarim*)
　　(*Bava Metzia* 76a).
A loaf of bread cost: 1 *pundion* (*Eruvin* 8, 2).
　　　　A cheap loaf: 1 *issar* (*Ib.* 7, 10).
1 *issar* could also buy a flask of oil (*B.M.* 5, 9).
1 *perutah* could buy: lamps and wicks (*Meila* 6, 3).
　　　　　　　　or: 1 citron (*Ib.* 6, 4).
　　　　　　　　or: 1 pomegranate (*Ib.*).
1 cloak or shirt could cost 3 *selaim* (*Ib.*).
A good quality cloak could cost double that — 1 golden
　　dinar (*Ib.*).
A dwelling could be rented for 1 *sela* per month
　　or ten *selaim* per year (*B.M.* 5, 2).
The rent of a bath-house (as a commercial undertaking)
　　could amount to 1 golden *dinar* per month (*B.M.* 8, 8).
A pair of oxen (for plowing) could cost 200 *zuz*
　　(*Bava Batra* 5, 1)
A house or a field could cost 1,000 *zuz* (*B.M.* 48a)

APPENDIX 3

סֵדֶר תַּנָּאִים וַאֲמוֹרָאִים

THE SEQUENCE OF TANNAIM AND AMORAIM

Two historical charts are appended. Chart 1 shows the main Tannaim during the period from Hillel to Rabbi Yehuda Ha-Nassi. (For the Tannaim before Hillel, see Pirkei Avot, ch.1.) Chart 2 shows the main Amoraim both in Eretz Yisrael and Babylon. (To provide continuity the bottom lines of Chart 1 have been repeated in the main at the top of Chart 2.)

The scale at the right of the charts shows the Jewish date and the corresponding Common Era date. It should be noted that the space allotted to different centuries is not always uniform. Personalities are placed on the charts in the position corresponding roughly with the assumed period of their main activity. Rabbi — Talmid and family relationships are shown and those who functioned as Nassi (President of the Sanhedrin, or Patriarch) are indicated by a symbol. All symbols are explained at the foot of Chart 2. Where the name of a sage's father appears in smaller type under the sage's name, this indicates that the sage is usually referred to by his own name alone. The place-names in brackets under some names refer to the place of main activity.

The alphabetical index of names which follows enables the student to locate any name on the two charts. The name required will be found either on the date-line indicated or immediately below it. (Ease of reference has been the criterion in selecting the date-lines in the two columns in the index, and the Jewish and civil dates shown there do not always correspond precisely.)

מַפְתֵּחַ לַתַּנָּאִים וַאֲמוֹרָאִים

לסה״נ C.E.	לבה״ע A.M.	מקום Place	תרשים Chart	
320	4080	א״י	2	ר׳ אבא
290	4050	א״י	2	ר׳ אבא בר זבדא
110	3870		1	אבא שאול
300	4050	א״י	2	ר׳ אבהו
210	3970	בבל	2	אבוה דשמואל
340	4100	בבל	2	אביי
280	4040	בבל	2	אבימי
220	3980		1, 2	ר׳ אושעיא
380	4140		2	רב אחא בריה דרב איקא
440	4200	בבל	2	רב אחא מדיפתי
220	3970		1, 2	אייבו
350	4100	בבל	2	רב איקא
90	3850		1	רבי אליעזר
60	3820		1	רבי אליעזר בן יעקב (א)
160	3920		1	רבי אליעזר בן יעקב (ב)
170	3930		1	ר׳ אליעזר בן ר׳ יוסי הגלילי
100	3860		1	ר׳ אלעזר המודעי
270	4030	א״י	2	ר׳ אלעזר בן פדת
100	3860		1	ר׳ אלעזר בן עזריה
90	3850		1	ר׳ אלעזר בן ערך
160	3920		1	ר׳ אלעזר בן שמוע
190	3950		1	ר׳ אלעזר ב״ר שמעון
130	3890		1	ר׳ אלעזר חסמא
280	4040	א״י	2	ר׳ אמי
380	4140	בבל	2	אמימר
280	4040	א״י	2	ר׳ אסי
400	4150	בבל	2	רב אשי
160	3920		1	ברוריה
200	3960	א״י	1	בר קפרא
20	3780		1	רבן גמליאל הזקן
90	3850		1	רבן גמליאל דיבנה
220	3980	א״י	1, 2	ר׳ גמליאל בן רבי
300	4050	א״י	2	רב דימי
270	4030	בבל	2	רב הונא
370	4130	בבל	2	רב הונא בריה דרב יהושע
— 40	3720		1	הלל
350	4110	א״י	2	ר׳ הלל
370	4130	בבל	2	רב זביד
440	4200	בבל	2	מר זוטרא

לסה"נ C.E.	לבה"ע A.M.	מקום Place	תרשים Chart	
310	4070	א"י	2	ר' זירא
330	4090	א"י	2	ר' חגי
240	4000	א"י	2	חזקיה
220	3980	א"י	1, 2	ר' חייא
280	4040	א"י	2	ר' חייא בר אבא
340	4100	בבל	2	רב חייא בר אבין
230	3990	א"י	1, 2	ר' חמא ב"ר חנינא
220	3980	א"י	1, 2	ר' חנינא בר חמא
70	3830		1	ר' חנינא בן דוסא
130	3890		1	ר' חנינא בן תרדיון
300	4060	בבל	2	רב חסדא
300	4060	א"י	2	ר' יוסי בר חנינא
100	3860		1	ר' טרפון
150	3910		1	ר' יאשיה (א)
270	4030	א"י	2	ר' יאשיה (ב)
440	4200	בבל	2	יהודה בר מרימר
160	3920		1	ר' יהודה
280	4040	בבל	2	רב יהודה
180	3940		1, 2	ר' יהודה הנשיא
240	4000	א"י	2	יהודה בן ר' חייא
250	4100	א"י	2	ר' יהודה נשיאה
90	3850		1	ר' יהושע
200	3950	א"י	1, 2	ר' יהושע בן לוי
250	4000	א"י	2	ר' יוחנן
100	3860		1	ר' יוחנן בן ברוקה
100	3860		1	ר' יוחנן בן נורי
50	3800		1	רבן יוחנן בן זכאי
280	4040	א"י	2	ר' יונה
150	3910		1	ר' יונתן
40	3800		1	יונתן בן הורכינס
30	3790		1	יונתן בן עוזיאל
160	3920		1	ר' יוסי
330	4090	א"י	2	ר' יוסי בר אבין
330	4090	א"י	2	ר' יוסי בר זבדא
190	3950		1	ר' יוסי ב"ר יהודה
120	3880		1	ר' יוסי הגלילי
310	4070	בבל	2	רב יוסף
280	4040	בבל	2	ילתא
300	4060	א"י	2	ר' יצחק
200	3960	א"י	1, 2	ר' יצחק בר אבדימי (א)
320	4080	בבל	2	ר' יצחק בר אבדימי (ב)
320	4080	א"י	2	ר' ירמיה

ר׳ ישמעאל	תרשים Chart	מקום Place	לבה״ע A.M.	לסה״נ C.E.
ר׳ ישמעאל	1		3880	120
ר׳ ישמעאל בנו של ר׳ יוסי הגלילי	1		3900	150
ר׳ ישמעאל ב״ר יוסי	1		3930	170
רב כהנא (א)	2	בבל	4010	250
רב כהנא (ב)	2	בבל	4140	380
לוי	1	א״י	3950	190
ר׳ מאיר	1		3920	160
מר בר רב אשי	2	בבל	4200	450
מר זוטרא	2	בבל	4170	410
מרימר	2	בבל	4180	420
מר עוקבא	2	בבל	3980	220
ר׳ נחמיה	1		3910	150
רב נחמן	2	בבל	4040	280
ר׳ נתן הבבלי	1		3940	180
סומכוס	1		3940	180
עולא	2	בבל	4060	310
ר׳ עקיבא	1		3880	120
ר׳ פנחס בן יאיר	1		3950	190
פלימו	1		3960	200
רב פפא	2	בבל	4120	360
רבי צדוק	1		3800	50
קרנא	2	בבל	4010	250
רב	2	בבל	3990	230
רבא	2	בבל	4100	340
רבה	2	בבל	4070	310
רבה בר בר חנה	2	א״י	4010	250
רבין	2	א״י	4060	300
רבינא (א)	2	בבל	4170	410
רבינא (ב)	2	בבל	4200	440
ריש לקיש	2	א״י	4020	260
רמי בר חמא	2	בבל	4100	340
רב שימי בר אשי	2	בבל	4140	380
שמואל	2	בבל	4000	240
רבן שמעון (א)	1		3750	10 —
רבן שמעון (ב)	1		3810	50
ר׳ שמעון בן אלעזר	1		3950	150
רבן שמעון בן גמליאל	1		3900	140
ר׳ שמעון בן יהוצדק	1		3960	200
ר׳ שמעון בן יוחאי	1		3920	160
ר׳ שמעון בן לקיש	2	א״י	4020	260
ר׳ שמעון בן מנסיא	1		3950	190
רב ששת	2	בבל	4070	310

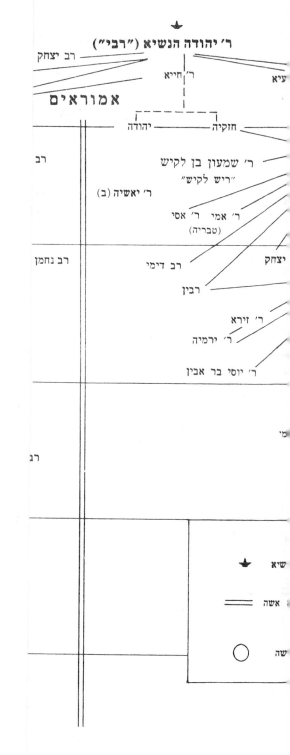

ר׳ יהודה הנשיא (״רבי״)

רב יצחק

ר׳ חייא

עיא

אמוראים

חזקיה ── יהודה

רב

ר׳ שמעון בן לקיש
״ריש לקיש״

ר׳ יאשיה (ב)

ר׳ אמי ר׳ אסי
(טבריה)

רב נחמן

רב דימי

יצחק

רבין

ר׳ זירא

ר׳ ירמיה

ר׳ יוסי בר אבין

מי

רג

שיא

אשה

שה

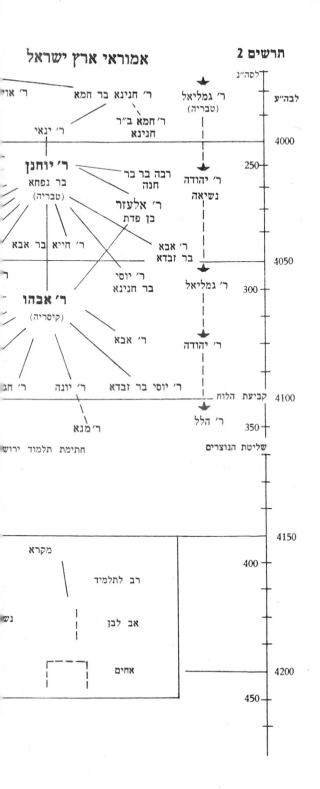

אמוראי ארץ ישראל

לספה״נ

לבה״ע

ר׳ גמליאל
(טבריה)

ר׳ אוי

ר׳ חנינא בר חמא

ר׳ חמא ב״ר
חנינא

ר׳ ינאי

4000

ר׳ יוחנן
בר נפחא
(טבריה)

רבה בר בר
חנה

ר׳ יהודה
נשיאה

250

ר׳ אלעזר
בן פדת

ר׳ חייא בר אבא

ר׳ אבא
בר זבדא

ר׳ אבא בר אבא

4050

ר׳

ר׳ יוסי
בר חנינא

ר׳ גמליאל

300

ר׳ אבהו
(קיסריה)

ר׳ אבא

ר׳ יהודה

ר׳ חג

ר׳ יונה

ר׳ יוסי בר זבדא

קביעת הלוח

4100

ר׳ מנא

ר׳ הלל

350

חתימת תלמוד ירוש

שליטת הנוצרים

4150

מקרא

400

רב לתלמיד

נש

אב לבן

אחים

4200

450